Criminal Justice
Recent Scholarship

Edited by
Marilyn McShane and Frank P. Williams III

A Series from LFB Scholarly

The Measurement of Crime
Victim Reporting and Police Recording

Shannan M. Catalano

LFB Scholarly Publishing LLC
New York 2006

Library of Congress Cataloging-in-Publication Data

Catalano, Shannan M.
  The measurement of crime : victim reporting and police recording /
Shannan M. Catalano.
     p. cm. -- (Criminal justice)
  Includes bibliographical references and index.
  ISBN 1-59332-155-4 (alk. paper)
  1. Victims of crimes surveys--United States. 2. Criminal statistics--
United States. 3. Victims of crimes--United States--Statistics. 4.
National crime victimization survey report. 5. Uniform crime reports
(Washington, D.C.) I. Title.
  HV6250.3.U5C39 2006
  362.88072'7--dc22

2006021760

ISBN 1-59332-155-4

Printed on acid-free 250-year-life paper.

Manufactured in the United States of America.

Table of Contents

List of Figures

List of Tables

Preface

This study uses data from the National Crime Victimization Survey (NCVS) and the Uniform Crime Reports (UCR) for the years 1973-2002 to examine the convergence between victim reporting and police recording of serious violent crime. For much of this thirty-year period the total volume of crime measured by the victimization survey is nearly double that recorded by official police statistics. Recently, however, the correspondence between the two trends has increased in a way suggesting that police are now recording all of the crimes reported to them by victims. This unprecedented convergence raises important methodological questions regarding public and official responses to crime over time. Important as well are the implications for broad empirical and methodological issues involved in the measurement of serious violent crime.

The results of this research indicate that changes in social perceptions of crime and a redesigned NCVS have contributed to increased correspondence between the two series. Specifically, changes in domestic violence legislation have contributed to increased police recording of aggravated assault while changes to the NCVS are negatively related to the increased correspondence in the reporting of rape. The implications of these findings and suggestion for future research are discussed.

Acknowledgements

Several individuals provided valuable support at various times during this research: Janet Lauritsen, Richard Rosenfeld, and Bryan Marshall. Their support was offered freely and frequently and contributed to the ultimate completion of this project. Special acknowledgement is extended to Janet Lauritsen for challenging me regarding the content and form of my argument and providing assistance in navigating the mysterious world of the National Crime Victimization Survey.

Much gratitude is extended to my family and friends for their support over the last several years. You are too many to list, but you all provided words of encouragement when needed most.

Many thanks to Leo Balk from LFB Scholarly for this opportunity, as well as the editors, Marilyn McShane and Frank P. Williams III. Much gratitude is also extended to Kay Hessemer for her editorial assistance.

CHAPTER 1

Victim Reporting and Police Recording

The level of crime in the United States is frequently used as one barometer of social well being. But, as a social phenomenon crime cannot be directly measured. Thus various means have evolved in an effort to understand the nature and extent of crime. Until thirty years ago the primary indicator of crime in the United States was the Uniform Crime Report (UCR), a yearly census of police agencies compiled by the Federal Bureau of Investigation (FBI). The UCR provides an official summary of the level of crime recorded by police agencies across the United States.

However, because the UCR represents an official summary of crime derived from the activities of law enforcement agencies, researchers have long questioned the accuracy of its portrayal for two reasons. First, questions arose as to whether an agency with a vested interest in crime was able to provide an objective assessment of crime. Second, early victimization studies suggested that not all crime was reported to the police by victims or witnesses. Hence, estimates of the volume and magnitude of unreported crime, often referred to as the "dark figure of crime," could only be speculative.

In 1973, partly in response to these criticisms, The National Crime Survey (NCS) was implemented nationwide. The survey was designed to elicit information from the victims of crime and ask questions regarding their experiences. In contrast to the UCR, the NCS was not restricted to crimes reported to the police. Additionally, the survey was initiated to measure the broader occurrence of crime and its correlates, not simply those known to enforcement agencies.

These differences in the volume of serious violent crime measured by the respective series are illustrated in Figure 1. In the last decade dramatic design changes have been implemented in both the NCS and the UCR. The UCR program is slowly undergoing a transition from a summary reporting format toward an incident based format known as the National Incident Based Reporting System (NIBRS). Full implementation is far from complete however and nationwide statistics remain available only through the UCR program. The NCS redesign went into effect in 1992 and has continued to gather victimization data as the National Crime Victimization Survey.[1] Taken together these two related crime measurement programs provide a picture of crime and changes in crime in the United States.

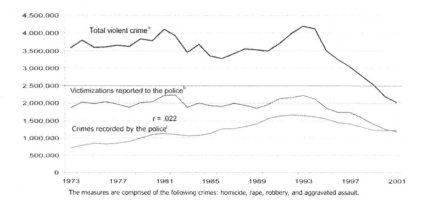

The measures are comprised of the following crimes: homicide, rape, robbery, and aggravated assault.

Figure 1. Measures of serious violent crime, 1973-2002

Source: [a,b]National Crime Victimization Survey, [b]Uniform Crime Reports

For much of this time period the total volume of crime measured by the victimization survey is nearly double that recorded by official statistics. Notable in Figure 1, however, is the behavior of the trends in the number of crimes reported by victims and that recorded by the police (United States Department of Justice, 2004a). Recently the two trends have converged in a way that suggests that police are now recording all of the victimizations that are reported to them (USDOJ, 2002a). Further in the year 2002, crimes recorded by the police actually exceeded reported crimes as measured by the National Crime Victimization Survey (NCVS). Indeed the two series have seemingly "converged" and are now "diverging" once more.[2] This correspondence between NCVS and UCR estimates is unprecedented and raises important questions regarding not only how the public responds to criminal experiences over time, but also how changing enforcement practices might have influenced the convergence.

Several factors might contribute to the increased correspondence between victim reporting and police recording of serious violent crime. For example, the UCR reflects all crimes recorded by the police in a given year. These recorded crimes result from (1) how often victims report crimes, and (2) how often the police record crimes (Langan and Farrington, 1996; Skogan, 1975, 1984). But many complaints coming to the attention of the police may not qualify as a criminal event. Problems may arise with insufficient evidence or the seriousness of the event may not meet legal standards for the police to act upon a complaint. The fact that the gap in reporting and recording of crimes has diminished in recent years suggests a fundamental change in police handling of crimes, changes in the nature of crimes reported to the police, or changing response to acts not previously perceived as crimes (Kitsuse and Cicourel, 1963; O'Brien, 1996; but see also Black 1970).

Three primary explanations may account for the recent convergence. First, increases in series correspondence may result from changes in police practices such as professionalization, the increased use of technology through electronic recording and computerization, and changes in procedural rules governing the handling of certain crimes (Langan and Farrington, 1998; Rand, Lynch, and Cantor, 1997; Langworthy, 1999). For the most part, the effect of such changes on long term NCVS and UCR convergence have not been empirically examined.

A second explanation is that demographic changes in the population have contributed to a change in the likelihood that victimizations will be reported to the police. Very little research has directly examined the influence of changing population characteristics on NCVS and UCR correspondence (see Biderman and Lynch, 1991). Decidedly more research has examined the relationship between demographic characteristics and offending (Cohen, Cantor, and Kluegal, 1981; Fox, 2000, 1996), victimization risk and subsequent willingness of victims to report crime to the police (Gottfredson and Hindelang, 1979; Hindelang, Gottfredson, and Garafolo, 1978), or the link between the two (Sampson and Lauritsen, 1990). Some of the population characteristics previous researchers identify include age, race, gender, and educational level to name but a few.

Lastly, changes in social attitudes may produce a greater sensitivity toward certain crimes (e.g. domestic violence) and empower the criminal justice system to respond to actions not previously thought to require formal intervention (Crowell and Burgess, 1996; Dugan, 2003, Dugan, Nagin, and Rosenfeld, 2003). Indeed, evidence suggests that police handling of certain offenses such as rape and assault is now different than in the past (Baumer, Felson, and Messner, 2003; Blumstein, 2000a, 2000b; Blumstein, 2000a, 2000b, 1998; Rosenfeld, 2004; see also Harris, Thomas, Fisher, and Hirsch, 2002) implying that a new broad scale agreement between the police and the public has emerged regarding the definition of criminal victimization. If social definitions of crime change, it seems plausible the effects would be reflected in both police handling and victim response, including reporting to law enforcement, to crime. Such effects may operate independently or interactively with demographic characteristics of the population or the manner in which police respond to crime.

Any of the three explanations may account for the recent convergence between what victims report and what police record. There is a final and fourth possible explanation for the observed convergence of the two series. In recent years, both the NCVS and UCR have undergone dramatic design change affecting the procedural and definitional aspects of how each series measures serious violent crime. In 1992, a redesigned NCVS was implemented, and during the same time frame the transition from a summary to incident-based measure of crime was implemented in the UCR. Though the transition to an incident-based measure of crime has not been fully implemented in the UCR, these changes may very well have influenced police recording practices in the normal UCR format. In light of the fact that both series have undergone these types of environmental changes, a fourth and as yet unexamined explanation is possible: increased correspondence between victim reporting and police recording is an artifact of attempts to redesign, or "upgrade," the manner in which the two programmatic series go about measuring crime.

CHAPTER 2

The Two Measures of Crime

THE UNIFORM CRIME REPORTS

The FBI's Uniform Crime Report (UCR) is the only source of national level data on police-recorded crimes over time. The UCR is the oldest ongoing collection of data on crime statistics in the United States. In 1929 the International Association of Chiefs of Police (IACP) convened a committee to discuss the implementation of a nationwide measure of crime. The committee undertook this project by first surveying local police departments in an effort to assess the most efficient way to summarize crime statistics. At this time it was decided that information could best be captured for violent and property crime that met two criteria. First, crimes had to be serious, and second, crimes had to be those most frequently reported to the police (Kincaid, 1984; Schneider and Wiersema, 1990). Seven crimes met these criteria and were chosen as an index of the level of crime in the United States.

Fluctuations in the level and magnitude of the index were seen as one way to measure changing patterns in criminality at a national level. The chosen crimes were both violent and non-violent in nature. These crimes included: murder and non-negligent manslaughter, forcible rapes, robbery, aggravated assault, larceny-theft, burglary, and motor vehicle theft. In 1970 the crime of arson was added to the index. During the first year of official recording in 1930, only 400 agencies across the United States participated in the program (Schneider and Wiersema, 1990), but by 2002, law enforcement agencies active in the UCR program represented approximately 288 million U.S. inhabitants, or 93.4% of the total population (Federal Bureau of Investigation, 2002).[3]

The UCR program is census-based which means that ideally all individual police agencies submit data on criminal activities they have recorded during a standard monthly reporting period. The statistics reported by the UCR cover all crimes committed against any person or entity in the country, including young children, visitors and foreign visitors, businesses, and organizations. Offenses are used to calculate, on a per capita basis, rates per 100,000 individuals in the population.

The UCR collects data in several areas, including offenses known to the police; property stolen and recovered; age, sex, race, and ethnic origin of persons arrested; and information on police employees. On a monthly basis summaries of these data are sent directly to the FBI by individual departments or are routed to a central clearinghouse within each state. Following tabulations and audit checks at the state level the data are forwarded to the FBI. Once received by the FBI, edit checks are performed to check for logical relationships amongst the data prior to release and dissemination to the public.

The basic unit of count for the UCR is the offense or crime event. For the crimes of rape and assault, the frequency of each offense will equal the number of victims; however, for the crimes of burglary and robbery, the number of offenses will be equal to the number of incidents. For example, if three men assault two women, this would be counted as two assault incidents. In contrast, if two individuals are robbed at gunpoint on the street this is counted as one offense, an armed robbery. Lastly, UCR crime counts represent only those crimes that are recorded by the police. A criminal incident may not be recorded for several reasons. Either the victim or individuals aware of the crime may not have reported the incident to the police. Alternately, the police may not file an official report for reasons such as lack of evidence.

Limitations of the UCR are generally related to error introduced through the reporting practices of jurisdictions. UCR data are collected monthly from participating jurisdictions and compiled into a yearly report of all crime known to and recorded by the police. This data is released to the public annually under the title *Crime in the United States* (CIUS). The original criteria for inclusion as outlined by the IACP—that is, the seriousness of the crime and frequency of reporting—required that a uniform definition of "crime" be applied to criminal events so that crime counts across jurisdictions would be comparable. To account for differences in the definitions of crime that vary by state the UCR instructs participating agencies to follow definitional guidelines supplied by the FBI rather than classify crime events according to local law or tradition (FBI, 1984). Incomplete reporting or the failure of submitted reports to adhere to the guidelines for completeness and accuracy as outlined by the FBI will introduce error in some quantity to the estimates of crime that are eventually published (Kincaid, 1984; Maltz and Targonski, 2002; Schneider and Wiersema, 1990).

Error in published numbers is also introduced when classification schemes are not followed properly or through the inaccurate application of counting guidelines. The basic counting unit of the UCR is the criminal offense, but when multiple criminal incidents occur during a single criminal offense, only the most serious crime is recorded and included in the UCR report. The "hierarchy rule," as this procedural guideline is known, stipulates that only the most serious crime in each incident report is tallied in the summary crime statistics forwarded to the FBI. Returning to the robbery example, if during the course of the crime one of the robbery victims is shot and killed by the offender, the crime is classified as a homicide rather than a robbery. The robbery incident is subsumed by the homicide and is not taken into consideration when the count for robberies is calculated for that parti-cular jurisdiction.

The hierarchy rule is identified as one of the limitations of the present UCR system because it constrains data to a summary format rather than a full accounting of incidents occurring during a criminal event. Research on the effect of the hierarchy rule produces inconsis-tent findings. Some research suggests that the hierarchy rule generates a nominal effect when applied to multiple offenses (Kincaid, 1984; see also Akiyama and Rosentahl, 1990), while other research suggests the rule obscures important contextual information regarding crimes (Maxfield, 1999; Thompson, Saltzman, and Bibel, 1999).

THE NATIONAL CRIME VICTIMIZATION SURVEY

The NCVS was first administered in 1972 and was designed to serve two purposes. First, the survey was intended to augment official statistics generated by law enforcement and second, to provide additional information on the characteristics of crime that were generally missing from official data (Penick and Owens, 1975; Sparks, 1981, 1976). In 1967, the President's Commission on Law Enforce-ment and the Administration of Justice suggested that "If we knew more about the characteristics of both offenders and victims, the nature of their relationships and the circumstances that create a high probability of criminal conduct, it seems likely that crime prevention and control programs could be made much more effective" (President's Commission, 2:1976).

The survey was developed to learn more about victim experiences as well as the characteristics of crime events. The crimes to be covered were those that would facilitate comparability with the UCR. Slight differences did exist, however. Homicide was excluded due to the victim-based nature of the survey. Both the UCR and NCVS record rape, robbery, and aggravated assault in their crime counts. The remaining crimes included in the NCVS are theft, burglary, and motor vehicle theft. In 1992 the crime of sexual assault was added to the survey as well. The NCVS does not include questions regarding arson.

The survey is sponsored by the Bureau of Justice Statistics (BJS) and conducted by the U.S. Department of the Census. The NCVS was designed with survey-based methodology, in contrast to the administrative recording framework of the UCR, and employs a probability-based sampling procedure. This type of procedure allows survey responses to be generalized to the population of United States residents aged 12 and older. The results of the survey are published annually by the BJS and are frequently the topic of intermittent special reports focusing on topical subjects.

As a survey of individuals, the NCVS solicits information from both victims and non-victims. This means that the survey is able to capture a wider range of information regarding experiences with crime. Most important, respondents who have been victims of crime are asked whether they reported their victimization to the police. Rates of reporting may then be generated for serious violent crimes, property crimes, and individual subclasses of crime. Questions are asked regarding crimes experienced by the household and individual household members. The crimes of burglary, theft, and motor vehicle theft are considered crimes against households. These are differentiated from the personal crimes of rape, sexual assault, robbery, and aggravated and simple assault experienced by individuals. One member of the household is generally surveyed regarding crimes against the entire household, and subsequently all individual members of the household twelve years of age or older are surveyed regarding their victimization experiences.

Individuals are selected to participate in the survey through a complex sampling procedure intended to provide a representative portrait of the larger population. A randomly chosen group of households is selected and interviewed twice per year for a period of three years regarding their experiences with victimization. At the end of this period, new households are rotated into the sample to replace exiting respondents.

Victimizations are calculated on a per capita basis as rates per 1,000 and are generated separately for crimes against individuals and crimes against households. In both instances, the base is weighted to reflect the actual U.S. population. The sampling procedure for the survey is household-based, thus the NCVS coverage is restricted to crimes against persons twelve and older that are tied to a household. The survey excludes crimes against young children, people without a permanent residence, businesses, and organizations.

Limitations of the NCVS are generally related to issues of error introduced by random sampling and non-sampling error. Sampling error refers to the possibility that statistical estimates are not representative of the general population. Non-sampling error refers to errors introduced during the interviewing process. For example, NCVS interviewers ask respondents to recall events within the preceding six-month time frame; however, occasionally respondents are unable to recall victimizations, especially if they occur frequently or are perpetrated by someone known to the victim. Another source of error is respondent fatigue. This term refers to the declining likelihood that victimizations will be reported during subsequent interviewing cycles. Respondent fatigue is cited as an additional limitation of the survey (Biderman and Lynch, 1991; Penick and Owens, 1976; Sparks, 1981).

Error is also introduced into victimization estimates through a procedure known as bounding. The bounding procedure is intended to limit victim recall error by asking respondents to remember victimization events within a certain time frame. Victims of a crime may "recall" a criminal event as happening within the previous six-month period when in actuality the event occurred outside of the six-month period. To minimize this type of error, the first interview of a respondent and household is used to bound subsequent interviews and reduce the chance that respondents will report duplicate victimization experiences.

To illustrate this concept, if a respondent reports a robbery in the first interview and again in the second interview, the NCVS interviewer may verify that these are indeed two separate events. Though bounding procedures reduce this form of error, the practice is tied to the household rather than individuals residing within the household. If household occupants move during the three-and-a-half year period they are in the sample, subsequent interviews of the household and individual respondents essentially become unbounded interviews. In turn this may create a situation where victimization experiences are inflated due to victim recall. Lastly, because the survey is probability–based, the extent of sampling errors is a function of the sample size and the relative rarity of a given victimization incident. This becomes increasingly problematic when rates of victimization are already low to begin with and are exacerbated for rare crimes such as rape.

NCVS AND UCR COMPARABILITY

The purpose of the UCR is to provide an accounting of all crimes known to the police. In contrast, the purpose of the NCVS is to provide information on the experiences of all crime victims whether or not their victimization was reported to the police. The crime coverage of the two systems varies as well. Though both data collection programs cover the crimes of rape, robbery, theft, burglary, and motor vehicle theft, the NCVS captures information on additional crimes, including simple and sexual assault. The UCR gathers data on the crimes of homicide and arson, crimes that the NCVS does not address.

Differences in population coverage between the two series are present as well. Unlike the UCR, the NCVS is not designed to capture information on crimes such as commercial robbery that are committed against businesses, establishments, or organizations. The UCR includes counts of crimes against all U.S. citizens, visitors, and illegal residents of any age. The NCVS includes crimes against households and individuals associated with those households who are twelve years of age and older.

Creating comparability requires that these issues of difference be reconciled. In the past, researchers have successfully created comparability between the two series so that meaningful analyses are possible (e.g., Biderman and Lynch, 1991; Blumstein, Cohen and Rosenfeld, 1991; Fox, 1996; Langan and Farrington, 1996). Indeed, Biderman and Lynch (1991) were the first to systematically examine and adjust for difference in scope, definition, and procedure between the two series. The first difference of scope arises because different rate bases are incorporated for the two series. The UCR uses the total resident population of the United States, while in contrast the NCVS uses the total population of the United States age 12 and older that are tied to a household. The homeless, individuals residing on military bases, and business are not counted in survey estimates. In the examination by Biderman and Lynch, NCVS household crimes—burglary and motor vehicle theft—were recalculated using the survey population as the base. Turning their attention to the UCR, the researchers truncated the UCR population base, for the same crime, to exclude the population under twelve years of age. These calculations brought the two NCVS and UCR estimates into closer proximity.

But rate bases account for only part of the discrepancy in NCVS and UCR estimates. Because the numerators of the rates for each series represent a crime count, any difference between the definitions of crime across the series will affect comparability. Such inter-series differences were accounted for by Biderman and Lynch (1991) by excluding crimes not reported to the police from the NCVS, omitting commercial crimes from the UCR, and restricting crimes to the most comparable between the two series: rape and aggravated assault.

COUNTING AND DEFINITIONS BETWEEN THE NCVS AND UCR

Further discrepancies arise from definitional and procedural nonconformities because the victimization survey distinguishes between a criminal victimization and a criminal incident. The purpose of the survey is to provide estimates of victimization on crimes of interest to the public (President's Commission, 1967). For purposes of the survey the focus remains on the single victimization as the unit of measure. A single victimization is defined as a specific criminal act that may involve one or more victims and one or more offenders. Each criminal victimization or incident is counted only once, by the most serious act that took place during the incident. For many specific categories of personal crime, victimizations will outnumber incidents because "[i]n any encounter involving a personal crime, more than one criminal act can be committed against an individual (Bureau of Justice Statistics, 1979).

This peculiarity results directly from two related contingencies. Some crime might be simultaneously committed against more than one person, and personal crimes may occur during the course of a commercial offense. Elaborating on this concept, if two customers are assaulted during the course of a store hold-up, the event is counted as a commercial robbery not an incident of personal assault. Additionally, an assault may precede a rape, but the criminal incident is counted only once by the most serious act, in this case a rape. This counting mechanism is similar to the one used by the FBI and ultimately facilitates comparisons of estimates between the two series, since the NCVS also applies a hierarchy rule when crimes co-occur. For both series the order of seriousness for personal crimes is (1) rape, (2) robbery and (3) aggravated assault.

In the study of personal crimes, especially violent crimes, victimization data are more appropriate than incident data. Victimization data allows for the contextualization of effects, reactions, and perceptions. In contrast incident data are better suited for explorations of the circumstances surrounding the occurrence of personal crime such as time and place, weapons, and the number of victims and offenders involved.

Due to the self-report nature of surveys, the NCVS is most successful in measuring crimes with victims who are able to understand what happened to them and how the victimization occurred, and who are willing to discuss the criminal event (Bureau of Justice Statistics, 1979). In contrast victimless crimes, crimes of which the victim is unaware, or crimes in which the victim participated are not well measured by the survey. The manner in which criminal incidents in the UCR are recorded stands apart from the NCVS in one important way. Whereas the crime survey emphasizes measurement of the victimization event, the police data direct greater attention toward the crime event. UCR protocols do, however, distinguish between crimes against persons versus crimes against property (FBI, 1985). Tables 1 and 2 summarize UCR and NCVS differences related to crime definitions, count protocols, and crime measurement.

Table 1. Crimes measured by the NCVS and UCR

UCR	NCVS
Homicide	—
Rape	Rape/sexual assault[a]
Robbery	Robbery
Aggravated assault	Aggravated assault
—	Simple assault
Theft	Theft
Burglary	Burglary
Motor vehicle theft	Motor vehicle theft
Arson	—

Source: Rand and Rennison (2002)

[a]   Rape and sexual assault were added to the survey in 1992.

Table 2. NCVS and UCR crime definitions and count protocol

Crime	Definition	Count
UCR		
Criminal homicide	The willful (nonnegligent) killing of one human being by another	Score one offense for each victim (crime against person)
Rape	The carnal knowledge of a female forcible and against her will	Score one offense for each victim (crime against person)
Robbery	the care, custody, or control of a person or persons by by force or threat of force or violence and/or by puttingthe victim in fear	Score one offense for each distinct operation (crime against property)
Aggravated assault	An unlawful attack by one person upon another	Score one offense per victim (crime against person)
NCVS		
Rape/sexual assault	Forced sexual intercourse, including both psychological coercion and physical force. Forced sexual intercourse means vaginal, anal, or oral penetration by the offender(s). This category included incidents where the penetration is from a foreign object such as a bottle. This definition includes attempted rapes, males and female victims, and heterosexual and homosexual rape	Score one per victimization
Robbery	of property or cash by force or threat of force, with or without a weapon, and with or without an injury.	Score one per victimization
Aggravated assault	Completed or attempted attack with a weapon, whether or not an injury occurred. It is also an attack without a weapon in which the victim is seriously injured.	Score one per victimization

Source: Federal Bureau of Investigation (1984).

CHAPTER 3

Explaining the Convergence

This research examines potential factors contributing to the convergence of crime reporting and police recording as evidenced by absolute crime counts in the NCVS and the UCR.[1] The principle question guiding this research is *what concomitant changes in victim reporting characteristics and police recording practices over the past thirty years contributed to the recent convergence between the nation's two measures of crime?* Four hypotheses are proffered: (1) changes in policing, (2) changes in the demographics of the U.S. population, (3) changes in social attitudes, and (4) methodological changes in the NCVS and UCR. The first two explanations have guided earlier research examining fluctuations in crime statistics. The third and fourth hypotheses remain to be empirically examined. Previous work and specific research questions related to the four explanations are now discussed in greater detail.

CHANGES IN POLICING

Fluctuations in reporting and recording over time may result from change in police recording practices. Between 1973 and 1990, the increased correspondence between victim reporting and police recording is primarily driven by relative increases in the level of police recording. From 1973 to 1995, levels of victim reporting increased 5 percent, while overall levels of police recording increased 116 percent (Rand, Lynch, and Cantor, 1997). And, by 1981, the difference between the NCVS and UCR was decreasing and appeared motivated by increases in police recording. What remains unknown, however, are the specific changes in policing behavior that led to this increase. Biderman and Lynch (1991) suggest that non-uniformity in the application of UCR procedures produced within-trend variation over time such that police recording practices of twenty years ago generated crime estimates that were dependent on factors other than levels of crime. Specifically, they examined the effect of an increasing number of civilians working in police departments in the 1970s, and find that for mid-size agencies the percentage of the workforce that is civilian is positively associated with an increased reporting of eligible events.

This influx of civilians led to an increasingly professionalized workforce that directly affected the daily activities of law enforcement agencies. Officers and agencies of thirty years ago were forced to place emphasis on certain crimes due to demands on their time and resources. This form of decision-making, known as discretion, reduced the ability of enforcement agencies to record all criminal activities brought to the attention of the police. Civilian employees generally functioned as administrative support staff in the role of dispatchers. Biderman and Lynch (1991) hypothesize that the higher proportion of civilian dispatchers reduced the level of street discretion by officers thus allowing for increased recording of crime.

Langan and Farrington (1998) expand on the police professionalization hypothesis and suggest five explanations that might account for administrative as well as policy-related change: (1) police have become more professional; (2) police operations have become more computerized; (3) calls to police are increasingly recorded electronically thus creating a trail; (4) police have become responsive to certain types of violence, such as domestic violence abuse and assault; and (5) agencies more frequently engage in defensive policing to preempt potential law suits.

The fourth and fifth hypotheses suggest that changes in recording may be generated from sources external to police organizations. Indeed, some scholars suggest that contemporary criminal justice, and all institutions for that matter, conducts business in constant observance of risk and potential risk (Ericson and Haggerty, 1997). The elements of risk in this context include all external threats to police organizations that will impact how the police go about the daily business of policing. Lawsuits stemming from improper use of force or negligence in responding to certain crimes may be transformed into a public spectacle, thus drawing attention away and distracting from the daily activities of law enforcement.

Yet well-known limitations of the UCR call into question the validity of the changes in policing explanation. For instance, the UCR has variable levels of state and agency participation over time (see

Maltz, 1999). Though some states provide statistics for nearly 100 percent of their agencies, other states such as Georgia, Mississippi, Vermont, and Tennessee fluctuate between 40 and 100 percent. Additionally, states such as Kentucky, Kansas, Montana, and New Hampshire have not contributed to the UCR data in recent years as a result of transitioning to the National Incident Based Reporting System (NIBRS) format. The state of Illinois is particularly troublesome. Due to definitional incompatibilities with regard to the crime of rape, the FBI has rejected all data submitted by the state since 1992 (Maltz, 1999). The problem of missing data and imputation are compounded, particularly at the county level. And though county-level data has previously been used (Lott, 1998, 2000; Lott and Mustard, 1997), some investigators remain wary of utilizing UCR data in this manner when the effect of imputation and missing data remains unknown (Maltz and Targonski, 2002).

Taken together, the above explanations widen the scope of the professionalization hypothesis to include factors influencing the broader administrative and organizational functions of the police. At the national level at least, even though police recording appears largely responsible for the observed convergence, this explanation is untested. Additionally, if the increased correspondence is attributable solely to changes in administrative and organizational capabilities of law enforcement agencies, the benefit of social policies enacted during the past thirty years is called into question. These changes in policy include legislation directed toward domestic violence, zero-tolerance order maintenance, community policing, and victim advocacy.

CHANGES IN POPULATION CHARACTERISTICS

Crimes become official statistics as the result of two related but distinct occurrences. First, a victim must report the crime to the police. Secondarily, the police response must be to record the crime by officially filing a report (Gottfredson and Gottfredson, 1980; Langan and Farrington, 1998). Hence, any variable influencing either the likelihood of victims' decisions to report or officers' decision to respond by officially filing a report, will alter the probability that a crime becomes an official statistic (see also Conaway and Lohr, 1994; Levitt, 1998).

Change in the demographic composition of the population will produce such an effect. As profiles of victims change, subsequent

responses to crime will change. Research examines a range of demographic characteristics associated with the nexus of victimization,
offending, and reporting of crime by victims. These characteristics are
age (Blumstein, 1995; Blumstein and Rosenfeld, 1995; Catalano, 2003;
Cohen and Land, 1987; O'Brien 1999a), gender (Catalano 2003;
Chilton, 1986; O'Brien, 1999b), and racial composition (Catalano,
2003; Chilton, 1986, 1987; Fox, 2000). Additionally, some research
suggests that as population characteristics change, crime rates them-
selves may change (Fox, 2000). In contrast, little research has
specifically examined the effect of demographic characteristics on
police recording of crime. Each of these variables presents a two part
consideration. First, certain group characteristics are associated with a
greater likelihood of reporting a crime to police. Second, certain group
characteristics are associated with an increased likelihood to be
involved in crime.

Though much individual research focuses on the separate factors,
Biderman and Lynch (1991) were among the first to simultaneously,
and exhaustively, explore the effects of age, race, and gender
composition on discrepancies between the NCVS and UCR over time.
Undeniably more theoretical leverage is gained by the knowledge that
these factors operate in tandem rather than singly (see especially
Hindelang, Gottfredson, and Garafolo, 1978). Their research showed
that (1) demographic changes in the population are associated with
changes in the likelihood that victims would report eligible crime
events, and (2) that demographic changes in the population are
associated with increased participation in criminal ventures by certain
high-risk subgroups. These changes are influential since they affect the
prevalence of reporting and the incidence of criminal victimization.

Yet, the greatest influence was generated not by age or the
interaction between age and race but from the changing racial
composition of the population. Biderman and Lynch (1991) generated
an estimate of the number of eligible events that may be reported to the
police for traditionally high and low reporting groups. Subsequently an
estimate was generated of the effect for a proportionate change of age
and race composition in these high and low reporting groups on the
number of crimes that were reported to the police. With these estimates
in hand they were able to calculate the extent to which these factors
increased correspondence between the two series. Three scenarios were
estimated for age, race, and an interaction between age and race.
Though controlling for age reduced inter-series discrepancies by

29 percent, the greatest effect was seen for race that reduced the discrepancy between the NCVS and UCR by 40 percent.

CHANGES IN THE PERCEPTION OF CRIME

Increased correspondence between the NCVS and UCR may represent an increased willingness to report by victims in conjunction with an increased ability to record crime by the police (Baumer, Felson, Messner, 2003; Conaway and Lohr, 1994; Gottfredson and Gottfredson, 1980; Gove, Hughes, and Geerken, 1985; see also Cohen and Felson; Cohen, Felson, and Land, 1980). Until approximately 1989, the increased correspondence appears driven by relative increases in rates of recording by the police, with relative rates of reporting to the police by victims relatively stable from 1973 to 1989.

Following the crime decline of the early 1990s, the increased correspondence is disproportionately influenced by a more rapidly declining number of reported crimes by victims than an increase in the number of recorded crimes by police. Indeed, the police recording of violent crime leveled off by 1999, while the number of victim-reported crimes continued to decline. Figure 2 presents the percentage of violent crime that victims state were reported to the police during the last thirty years. Though relatively stable between 50 and 60 percent, the crimes that victims are reporting to police have steadily increased since 1995, contributing to the recent convergence.

One explanation is that over time a greater fraction of the crimes reported by victims are eligible to be recorded by police. That is, broader based social changes may contribute to greater correspondence because perceptions and willingness to engage the police are changing over time or because police response to certain crimes is changing over time (Martin, 1995; Reiss, 1967; Reiss and Roth, 1993; Rosenfeld, 2000; Sherman, 1992, 1984). Referring to Figure 1, observe that following the crime decline beginning in the early 1990s increasing correspondence is less influenced by increases in recording than by a decreasing rate of reporting.

Figure 2 shows that victims were reporting a higher percentage of crimes at the same time that overall levels of crime in the United States were declining (Hart and Rennison, 2003). Though victims were reporting less crime overall, the crimes that they did report were those that continued to be eligible for recording by the police. This might suggest greater agreement regarding definitions of crime, views of violence, and the handling of crime between the public and police. Yet because levels of victim reporting fluctuate between 50 and 60 percent, there is reason to suspect that the convergence may be a temporary artifact of changing social processes rather than evidence of a long-term social change. The effects of these explanations remain unexamined.

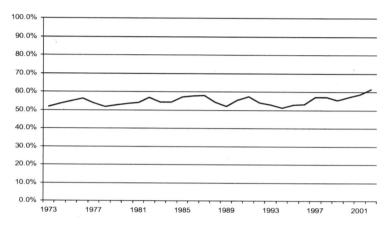

**Figure 2. Percent of serious violent crime reported to the
     police, 1973-2002**

Note: Serious violent crime is comprised of the following crimes: homicide, rape, robbery, and aggravated assault.

Source: National Crime Victimization Survey and Uniform Crime Report.

Moreover, an important question is whether, when disaggregated, certain crime subclasses exert a greater or lesser influence on the observed correspondence. The effects of individual crime types are often masked when examining crime trends in the aggregate (Blumstein 2000a, 2000b, 1995). This dynamic may be explored in greater detail by examining the frequency with which police record certain offenses as compared to offenses victims state were reported to police. Such an analysis is required to test the assertion that police or victim perceptions of crime have changed and become increasingly sensitive to classification, reporting, and recording.

Crimes such as assault that relate specifically to domestic violence, and offenses punishable by three-strikes legislation may play proxy to shifts in public perceptions regarding crime. This will occur through a differential treatment of such offenses by enforcement officers and the citizenry. The underlying argument here is that as the understanding of certain crimes changes broadly, both police and the public will respond differently when exposed to these incidents. In turn, such differential reactions will influence the correspondence between victimizations reported to the police and recorded criminal incidents reflected in UCR administrative records. Though this issue has not been directly addressed in the research literature, studies examining changing police response to certain criminal offenses are encouraging (Parks, 1976).

For instance, reporting of rape increased dramatically during the 1970s and 1980s. Increased reporting for this crime is seen primarily in rapes committed by husbands, ex-husbands, and non-strangers (Baumer, Felson, and Messner, 2003). This clearly represents a shift from a previous time where rape was rarely addressed in the criminal context (Brownmiller, 1975). Indeed, the 1960s and 1970s were eras characterized by greater awareness toward racial and gender equality. The 1970s, particularly, were awash in public awareness campaigns and reforms aimed at the protection and treatment of women (Brownmiller, 1975). High-visibility campaigns and grassroots movements specifically targeted the crimes of rape and domestic battery (Bienen, 1988; Berger, Searles, and Neuman, 1994; see also Brownmiller, 1975).

In contrast to the relative rarity of rape as a criminal event, intimate partner and familial violence more frequently manifests as simple or aggravated assault, and is always committed by an offender known to the victim (Durose, Harlow, Langan, Motivans, Rantala, and Smith, 2005). Research suggests that notable declines in intimate partner homicide between 1976-1996 is associated with legislation directed toward resources designed to prevent overall intimate partner violence (Dugan, Nagin, and Rosenfeld, 2003). One study found that more aggressive arrest tactics, including mandatory arrest, were associated with fewer killings, while increased dispensation of protection orders by prosecutors' offices were associated with an increase in homicides of white women (married and non-married) as well as unmarried black females (Dugan, Nagin, and Rosenfeld, 2003). Particularly interesting is that some resources are conversely related to higher levels of homicide.

Germane in the current context is the realization that legislative mandates reflect fundamental shifts in the perception of intimate partner violence from a once-personal or family matter to an offense warranting state intervention. Relevant from a social standpoint is that prevention and interventionist tactics have been brought to bear on the issue of intimate partner violence and that these tactics have affected crime statistics at the national level.

These shifting social perceptions and reactions operate independently of law enforcement and public demographics. The implementation of policies or social awareness toward specific crimes, such as violence by intimates, may lead to changes in the level of reporting for those victimizations. Presumably enforcement responses have changed as well, though specific types of events (i.e. rape, robbery, and aggravated assault) may exert a greater or lesser effect on the convergence between reported victimizations and recorded police statistics. If so, police recording of certain offenses will motivate convergence between the two series.

CHANGES IN METHODOLOGICAL DESIGN

Lastly, the convergence may be an artifact of redesign in the NCVS and UCR. Both systems have undergone methodological revisions. In some instances the modifications were intended to increase precision of the data collection effort; however, other adjustments arose from financial considerations (Lauritsen, 2005).

Research on this topic is both cross-sectional and longitudinal in nature, with much research working toward the reduction of observable differences in the estimates of crime measured by the NCVS and UCR (Biderman and Lynch, 1991; Blumstein, Cohen, Rosenfeld, 1991; Cohen and Land, 1984; Cohen and Lichbach, 1984; Hindelang, Hirschi, and Weis, 1979; Jensen and Karpos, 1993; Langan and Farrington, 1998; McDowall and Loftin, 1992; Menard, 1992, 1992, 19991; O'Brien, 1996, 1991, 1990; O'Brien, Schicor, and Decker, 1980).

Many of these studies are prompted by the implied notion that NCVS and UCR equality *should* exist, or that comparability may be achieved through various forms of statistical fine-tuning. In many respects, these endeavors were prompted from what Biderman and Lynch (1991) term the "Let's you and him fight!" mentality between the NCVS, UCR, and outside sources such as the media. As the nation's two indicators of crime, both programmatic series are frequently expected to provide identical estimates of crime. But absolute correspondence between the two series is impossible without first minimizing NCVS/UCR differences.

METHODOLOGICAL CHANGE IN THE UCR

The UCR is limited by the application of the , since its application obscures the detailed characteristics of criminal events in which more than one offense occurs. Additionally, the summary-based nature of UCR administrative records means crime counts from each reporting agency become the unit of analysis. Thus, researchers wishing to conduct investigations into crime using UCR data are restricted to analyzing crime totals reported by each agency (Maxfield, 1999).

UCR redesign efforts are directed toward shifting from a summary-based format to an incident-based reporting system known as the National Incident Based Reporting System (NIBRS). Incident-based crime records will allow multiple incidents within a crime event to be extracted and analyzed either separately or as a component in the constellation of the crime event. Such an overhaul of police statistics would be a boon for practitioners, researchers, and the public more generally. However, implementation of the NIBRS at the national level is slow. As of 2003, only 23 states were reporting under the new incident-based format (Bureau of Justice Statistics, 2006).

Full implementation of NIBRS may never occur at the national level. This form of police recording currently covers only 16 percent of the United States population. But ancillary attention generated by NIBRS may have unexpectedly contributed to better record-keeping amongst reporting agencies utilizing the UCR recording format. Again, a long-term upward trend in police recording is in evidence prior to the implementation of NIBRS in the early 1990s.

METHODOLOGICAL CHANGE IN THE NCVS

The majority of extensively documented methodological changes have been made to the victimization survey. These changes are discussed next.

Mode of interviewing

In the 1970s, nearly all NCVS respondents were interviewed in person. But as a result of budgetary constraints, over time a greater proportion of interviews were conducted by telephone beginning in the late 1970s. Computer Assisted Telephone Interviewing (CATI) began as a test in the late 1980s and was introduced on a broad scale with the Redesign in 1992 (Groves and Nicholls, 1986; House, 1985; Hubble and Wilder, 1995). The percentage of telephone interviewing varies between 20 and 80 percent over the past thirty years. Currently 75 percent of all NCVS interviews are administered via telephone. The percentage of CATI shows similar increases, from 0 prior to the 1980s increasing to between 20 and 40 percentage points after the Redesign.

Research on the effect of telephone versus in-person interviewing is mixed, with some research indicating little impact on survey estimates (Roman and Sliwa, 1982), while contradictory research suggests that estimates will differ based on crime type and population subgroup. CATI is associated with the increased reporting of events due to the reduction of interviewer error when following skip patterns within the electronic instrument (Hubble and Wilder, 1995; Groves and Couper, 1998). In recent years the advent of telephone options such as call blocking and caller identification translate to a decreased ability to reach frequently reluctant participants (Groves and Couper, 1998; Oldendick, 1993). This essentially negates any benefit derived from the format. In entirety research on the effect of increased CATI and telephone usage remains murky at best, and to date no research directly examines the influence of increased telephone and CATI usage in the production of national level crime estimates (Monahan, 2005).

Response rates

In the early years of the crime survey, response rates for both persons and households hovered near 100 percent, but within the last ten years, person response rates for the survey declined from approximately 99 to 86 percent. Though not as drastic, household response rates have similarly declined from approximately 96 percent in 1973 to 92 percent in 2002.

The NCVS instrument is administered by the Department of the Census, which is known for producing extremely high survey participation rates among households and individuals. The Census Bureau adjusts for non-response amongst participants through the use of weighting procedure. Weighting is a common survey practice in which individual responses are multiplied by a factor so as to provide an estimate equivalent to the population under examination. As non-response amongst survey participants increases, weights are applied to compensate for the decreased number of compliant respondents. The effect of long term declining response rates on estimated victimization rates remains unknown. It is unclear (and the subject of much debate) the level at which weighting of data ceases to provide a representative reflection of the larger population and to date there is little consensus on the subject (see Groves and Couper, 1998).

Unfortunately for the victimization survey, declining response rates are associated with groups at the highest risk of violent victimization: the young, poor, and transient. In this case, regardless of weights applied, as fewer individuals participate in the survey, the burden of representation falls on a decreasing number of compliant survey responders. Such effects are substantial for certain subgroups of the population; however, the effects on crime rates for the general population are likely not great since subgroups comprise a small portion of the overall population (Cohen, 2006).

Additionally, lower survey response rates for high risk groups may produce unknown effects for estimates as crime incidence in general declines, especially for relatively rare offenses such as rape or robbery (Atrostic, Bates, Burt, and Silberstein, 2001; Groves, 1989; Groves and Couper, 1998; but see also Smith, 1995; DeHeer, 1999). The empirical literature supports the proposition that survey nonresponse is an undesirable but tolerable aspect of survey research (Groves and Couper, 1998; Steeh, Kirgis, Cannon, and DeWitt, 2001). The level of acceptable response generally varies depending on the methodological preference of the researcher and the purpose of the survey (Steeh, Kirgis, Cannon, and DeWitt, 2001).

Unbounded interviews

An important characteristic of the NCVS is that bounding is used to limit the "telescoping" of crime events into the reference period. Seven interviews are conducted for each household sampled in the survey. After the first interview in a household, prior interviews are used to "bound" subsequent interviews. Early research on the effect of unbounded interviews suggests that interviews not temporally bounded are characterized by inflated estimates (Biderman and Cantor, 1984; Biderman et al., 1986; Penick and Owens, 1976).

This occurs for two reasons, the first of which is telescoping. The second reason stems from the fact that bounding status is correlated with residential mobility, which is in turn correlated with criminal victimization. Individuals at the highest risk of victimization are very transient, and bounding in the NCVS is tied to a household rather than residents residing within a household (Dugan, 1999; Hindelang, Gottfredson, and Garofalo, 1978; Penick and Owen, 1976).

This nuance of the survey means that first-time interviews with members of replacement households, i.e. households moving into units vacated by NCVS respondents, are not bounded by previous interviews but are included in victimization estimates. The inclusion of these participants may potentially generate inflated estimates that vary depending on whether mobility amongst the population is increasing or decreasing (Addington, 2005; Biderman and lynch, 1991; Dugan, 1999). This type of bounding procedure has the potential to affect the NCVS trend because the presence of unbounded interviews in the NCVS has fluctuated between 10.7 and 14.7 percentage points during the course of the survey.

Proxy interviews

Proxy interviews refer to the practice of interviewing eligible respondents through a proxy, or available adult within the sampled household. Between 1973 and 1986 the majority of proxy interviews were conducted for 12- and 13-year-olds, because Census had a policy of not directly interviewing household members of this age. However, beginning in 1986, children of these ages were interviewed directly in the NCVS. Proxy interviews were implemented within the survey for two reasons. During the developmental stage of the NCVS research it was believed that children were cognitively unable to comprehend and respond to questions regarding victimization, and additionally, that parents would object to the questioning of children regarding the sensitive topic of victimization (Rand, 2005).

In 1974 a test of proxy interviewing was conducted in San Francisco to evaluate the feasibility of interviewing children under the age of 13 directly rather than through the proxy format The results indicated that slightly higher victimization rates were reported in the self-response format, with children reporting higher rates of minor events such as simple assault and petty theft (Gray, 1974; Rand 1974). Anecdotal accounts suggested that children were unlikely to report these minor events to adults because the event was viewed as insignificant and the child simply forgot until prompted directly (Gray, 1974).

The validity of these results was initially called into question due to the small sample tested (Turner, 1974). However subsequent research supported the proposition that those incidents of victimization were substantially underreported using a proxy-interviewing format (Reiss, 1982). Lastly, adults within tested households did not object to the type of survey questions asked of youngsters during the San Francisco test. Ultimately, the decision to use a direct interviewing format for 12- and 13- year-olds was based on the second finding (Gray, 1974; Rand, 2005, 1974, Klaus, 2005).

Questionnaire

In a 1976 review of the NCVS predecessor, the National Academy of Science recommended that several aspects of the survey be improved. The Academy specifically suggested that an improved screening section might better stimulate victim recall of crime and help reduce the subjectivity often associated with certain survey questions. For example victims often downplayed victimizations if the offender was an intimate or an acquaintance. Once implemented, the enhanced screening questions improved the measurement of traditionally underreported crimes such as rape and those committed by acquaintances, family members, and intimates (Biderman et al., 1986; Kinderman, Lynch, Cantor, 1997; Penick and Owen, 1976). Higher counts of rape and aggravated assaults were reported, though robbery showed no appreciable change. In general, the available evidence suggests the questionnaire redesign produced the desired effect (Kindermann, Lynch, and Cantor, 1997). Not only were victims of crime able to recall victimizations that were reported to the police, but the recalled events included the offenses of rape and aggravated assault that were less likely to be captured in the previous surveys.

CHAPTER 4

Potential Factors Contributing to Convergence

An empirical examination of convergence requires three characteristics of the data. These include a time series of serious violent crime spanning 1973-2002 that is disaggregated for the crimes of rape, robbery, and aggravated assault. Neither the NCVS nor the UCR provides additional data that allow for hypothesis testing. Hence a third requirement for analysis is the inclusion of appropriate longitudinal variables to test the hypotheses proposed by the research questions. Regardless of purpose, all data for this study are derived from secondary sources. Dependent variables are generated from estimates of crime as reported by victims or third parties (see Planty, 2002) and recorded by police from 1973-2002. Independent variables are related to changes in policing practice, demographic population characteristics, changing social perceptions of criminal violence, and UCR and NCVS methodological design change.

These data are generated from the NCVS, the UCR, Law Enforcement Management and Administration Statistics Project (LEMAS), The Sourcebook of Criminal Justice Statistics (Sourcebook), The United States Department of Census, the General Social Survey (GSS), the NIBRS, and national-level data on domestic violence (Dugan, Nagin, and Rosenfeld, 2003). Table 3 presents the data sources from which dependent and independent variables are constructed.

Table 3. Data sources used in the current research

UCR	Uniform Crime Report
NIBRS	National Incident Based Reporting System
NCVS	National Crime (Victimization) Survey
LEMAS	Law Enforcement Management and Administrative Statistics
Sourcebook	Sourcebook of Criminal Justice Statistics
Census	United States Bureau of the Census
GSS	General Social Survey
Domestic violence	Dugan, Nagin, and Rosenfeld (2003)

Tables 4 and 5 in the following section provide roadmaps for the manner in which the dependent and explanatory variables are constructed. Additionally, each table provides a numerical reference to Appendix 1, which contains graphs of the variables discussed below. Prior to discussing dependent and independent variables, crime category groupings within the NCVS over time must be addressed.

DISAGGREGATED NCVS MEASURES

The BJS releases annual victimization estimates. Prior to 1995 this document was simply titled *Criminal Victimization* with the specific year following. From 1995 onward, the document has been titled Criminal Victimization in the United States. Regardless of title, the document has informally been referred to as the "tome," a name that harkens back to the days when the BJS was a component of the now-defunct Law Enforcement Assistance Administration (LEAA). During this time any lengthy document was referred to as a tome. The data used in the current project are derived from these tomes.

Due to changes in the NCS and later the NCVS, variation exists in the presentation of disaggregated crime types across years. For example, prior to 1985 NCS estimates are presented in a manner making it impossible to calculate estimates of attempted versus completed crimes for rape, robbery, and aggravated assault. This in turn prohibits the calculation of a total estimate for completed and attempted crimes of serious violence. In contrast, from 1985 onward attempted and completed victimization estimates are presented for overall crimes of violence, rape, robbery, and aggravated assault. Though the definitions for each crime type are stable since 1973, the ability to generate more distinctive sub-categories of victimizations is not consistent across the study period. A brief discussion of these changes and implications for the current study is now presented.

For the crime of rape the following applies: from 1973-1984 an estimate labeled "rape and attempted rape" is presented. Though not specifically stated, the estimate captures both completed and attempted rapes reported by victims. However, beginning in 1985 the crime of rape is presented as an aggregated total that is then further disaggregated into both completed and attempted categories. When combined with other categories of completed and attempted crimes, the disaggregated estimates of rape may be used to calculate overall estimates of completed and attempted crimes of violence.

A third change in the rape category occurred in 1993 with the full implementation of the newly redesigned NCVS. One of the goals of the redesign was to expand the scope of crimes covered (Kinderman, Lynch, and Cantor, 1997; Taylor 1989). Thus in 1993, a new offense category was introduced that captured both rape and sexual assault. For example, a total estimate for attempted and completed rape is presented, and then this aggregate is further separated into attempted and completed categories. An estimate for sexual assault is presented, though there is no distinction between completed and attempted victimizations.

A similar change occurs in the presentation of robbery estimates. As with all other crime categories, a total estimate for robbery victimizations is presented. The difference lies in the manner that the victimization is disaggregated. Between 1973 and 1985, robbery victimizations are partitioned into three categories designed to emphasize injury versus non-injury events. A category titled "robbery and attempted robbery with injury" provides estimates of all injury-related robbery victimizations. Yet this category is not broken down into attempted and completed victimization with injury. Instead, the category is disaggregated into serious and minor injury-related events. Thus there is no way to discern how many of these injury-related events were completed or attempted. A second category, "robbery without injury," provides an estimate of all completed robberies that occurred without an injury. Lastly, a third category, "attempted robbery without an injury" represents all remaining robbery victimizations that were attempted without injury.

As with the rape category, a change in the presentation of robbery estimates occurred in 1985. Robbery victimizations are now presented in two main categories, (1) completed, and (2) attempted. Victimization estimates are presented as totals for each category, and within each category these estimates are further broken down into events occurring with and without an injury. Similar to the example of rape, the new categories provide researchers with the ability to generate overall estimates of completed and attempted crimes of violence. Prior to 1985 this was not possible due to the emphasis on injury versus non-injury events. For aggravated assault the change is subtler. From 1973 to 1984, the aggravated assault category is disaggregated into aggravated assaults with injury and aggravated assaults attempted with a weapon. Beginning in 1985, aggravated assaults are disaggregated into incidents completed with injury ant incidents attempted with a weapon.

Crimes of violence first appear as the component parts of completed and attempted incidents in 1985. Though a pre-1985 measure for total crimes of violence can be computed by summing violent crime categories, comparable categories for completed and attempted crimes of violence cannot be computed because of the reclassification of rape and aggravated assault post-1985 (see Baumer, Felson, and Messner, 2003 for a detailed explication of changes in rape classification).

Previous research suggests that completed crimes of violence are more likely to be reported to the police and thus become part of the official record (Gove, Hughes, and Geerken, 1985; Menard and Covey 1988; Skogan, 1976). Considering the current research question, this approach would be useful. Though it is possible to generate separate completed and attempted categories for the three categories, generating these estimates would require extraction and reclassification of the data from the original NCS files for the years 1973-1984. For the category of robbery victimization by injury or non-injury is possible. However, although this approach may be useful in discerning those events with an increased likelihood of being reported (Menard and Covey, 1988), the current project focuses on the increased congruence between victim reporting and police recording that has already occurred.

Additionally, data derived from the BJS already provide a measure for total crimes of violence, and the distinction between attempted and completed events, as with robbery, is of less import for the present study. Comparable UCR counts for these crimes combine both attempted and completed incidents. In light of these considerations, for the categories of rape and attempted rape, robbery, and aggravated assault the total yearly victimization estimate presented in the NCVS tome are used.

DEPENDENT VARIABLES

The dependent variables for this study are generated from the NCVS and UCR. Reports of victimizations are derived from the NCVS. Police recording data are derived from the UCR. This study uses the raw count of crimes as recorded by the two data collection programs rather than rates because of programmatic differences in how each of the programs calculates crime rates at the national level.

Four variations of the dependent variables were constructed for preliminary examination in this study. In each case an aggregate variable captures all serious violent crime together: homicide added to the NCVS, rape, robbery and aggravated assault. Table 4 presents a listing of the dependent variables included in this study.

Table 4. Construction of dependent variables

Measure	Construction	Appendix 1 Reference
Police-recorded Crime		
Aggregated Measure (homicide, rape, robbery, assault)	BJS	Graph 1
Disaggregated Measure		
rape	UCR	Graph 2
robbery	UCR	Graph 3
aggravated assault	UCR 1973-2002	Graph 4
Victim-reported Crime		
Aggregated Measure (homicide, rape, robbery, assault)	BJS	Graph 1
Disaggregated Measure		
rape	NCVS	Graph 2
robbery	NCVS	Graph 3
aggravated assault	NCVS	Graph 4
Percentage recorded to reported SVC		
aggregate measure	UCR crime count divided by NCVS-reported crime count multiplied by 100	Graph 6
rape		Graph 7
robbery		Graph 8
aggravated assault		Graph 9
Difference of recorded to reported		
aggregate measure	UCR crime count minus NCVS crime count	Graph 10
rape		Graph 11
robbery		Graph 12
aggravated assault		Graph 13
Percent change score recorded to reported		
aggregate measure	([time 2-time1]/time 2)*-100)	Graph 14
rape		Graph 15
robbery		Graph 16
aggravated assault		Graph 17

Measure	Construction	Appendix 1 Reference
Percent change score difference recorded to reported		
aggregate measure		Graph 18
rape	([time 2-time1]/time 2)*-100)	Graph 19
robbery	([time 2-time1]/time 2)*-100)	Graph 20
aggravated assault	([time 2-time1]/time 2)*-100)	Graph 21

BJS - Bureau of Justice Statistics (2002).
UCR - Uniform Crime Reports, 1973-2002.
NCVS - National Crime Victimization Survey, 1973-2002.

Graphs 1-4 of Appendix 1 present the raw count of crime occurrences derived from the NCVS and UCR. Graph 5 presents all the counts simultaneously for comparative purposes. The first dependent variable is constructed as the percentage of UCR crimes reflected in the count of NCVS crimes that were reported to the police. This is presented in Graphs 6-9. The second dependent variable, shown in Graphs 10-13, is constructed as a difference score between the two series. The third form of the dependent variable, presented in Graphs 14-17, is constructed as a percent change score for the percentage of UCR crimes reflected in the NCVS crime counts. Lastly, a similar percent change score is constructed for the difference score between NCVS and UCR crime counts and is presented in Graphs 18-21 of Appendix 1.

Recall that Graph 1 presents the trend lines for all serious violent crime from 1973-2002. For the majority of this time period there is a nearly 50 percent differential between the amount of serious violent crime measured by the NCVS and the UCR. During the 1980s the trend line for police-recorded crimes begins to increase while the NCVS-reported crimes remains relatively stable. Graphs 2-4 present the crimes in a disaggregated format for rape, robbery, and aggravated assault. For the crime of rape, the trend shows a steady increase over time for police-recorded instances of this crime. In comparison, the trend line for victim reporting shows extreme fluctuations, likely due to the relative rarity of this crime and the inability of the survey to precisely measure this crime in light of diminishing sample size.

Graph 3 presents the counts of robbery recorded by police and victimizations reported to the police. The behavior of these trends is more similar than for any other crime type. The NCVS closely mimics its UCR counterpart with steady increases and decreases over time. As with rape, in recent years the UCR records more robberies than are captured by NCVS estimates.

Lastly, Graph 4 presents counts of recorded and reported aggravated assault for the two series. Prior to 1989, victims reported more than twice the number of crimes recorded in the UCR. However while the UCR crime counts have been steadily increasing, NCVS counts remained relatively stable until 1990, at which time they began to drop. Although the UCR is recording a relatively stable number of these crimes, victims are reporting fewer of these types of crime over the past ten years and possibly contributing to the increased correspondence in this manner.

EXPLANATORY VARIABLES

Table 5 presents a full listing of the explanatory variables included in this study.

Policing

Data on changes in policing are derived from several sources. Nationally representative data on the police is only recently available through the BJS sponsored Law Enforcement Administration Statistics (LEMAS) project. Though a rich source of data, LEMAS is available only from 1987 forward. Additional measures can be compiled from different sources such as the UCR and NIBRS. For example, Biderman and Lynch (1991) use the yearly percentage of the civilian workforce in enforcement agencies as one measure of organizational change over time. Changing organization structure may also be measured by the extent of NIBRS coverage across the United States. These sources of data may all be used to capture structural and procedural changes over time. Additional sources of data on policing variables are now discussed.

Table 5. Explanatory variables generated and explored for possible use

Variable	Construction	Appendix 1 Reference
NCVS		
Population under 12	% population less than 12 years of age	Graph 34
Person response rate	% responding to survey	Graph 35
CATI	% CATI interviews	Graph 36
Telephone	% telephone interviews	Graph 37
Primary sampling unit reduction	(0=no; 1=yes)	Graph 38
Proxy interview for under 12 years of age	(0=no; 1=yes)	Graph 39
NCVS redesign	(0=pre-redesign; 1=post-redesign)	Graph 40
Unbounded interviews	Percent new households in sampling frame	Graph 41
SVC- series victimizations	% of series victimizations included in estimate	Graph 42
Rape- series victimizations	% of series victimizations included in estimate	Graph 43
Robbery- series victimizations	% of series victimizations included in estimate	Graph 44
Aggravated assault- series victimizations	% of series victimizations included in estimate	Graph 45
12+ population base	Census generated number of 12+ in U.S. population	Graph 46
Total population under 12 years of age	Number of individuals in U.S. population	Graph 47
Household population base	Census generated number of U.S. households	Graph 48
Persons interviewed	Number of persons surveyed annually	Graph 49
Sampled households	Households sampled for survey annually	Graph 50
Household response rate	% of households responding to survey	Graph 51
% svc reported	% of all svc reported to police	Graph 52
% rape reported	% of all rape reported to police	Graph 53
% robbery reported	% of all robber reported to police	Graph 54
% aggravated assault reported	% of all aggravated assault reported to police	Graph 55
% simple assault reported	% of all simple assault reported to police	Graph 56

Variable	Construction	Appendix 1 Reference
LEMAS		
Total sampling frame	actual agencies sampled	Graph 57
Agency total weighted	total U.S. agencies weighted	Graph 58
Officer total weighted	total officers weighted	Graph 59
Survey response rate	agency response rate	Graph 60
Percent minority officers	percent minorities employed	Graph 61
Education requirement	% agencies requiring some education	Graph 62
Basic 911 participation	% with minimal 911 capabilities	Graph 63
911	% using expanded 911	Graph 64
Civilians employed	Number of civilians employed	Graph 65
Officer total for local police departments only	Number employed by local agencies only	Graph 66
Number civilians in local agencies	Number employed by local agencies only	Graph 67
Total number civilians local agencies	Raw count of employed civilians	Graph 68
Number of local police departments	Total number weighted	Graph 69
Computers for record keeping	% using computers for record keeping	Graph 70
Computers for criminal investigation	% of agencies using computers for investigation	Graph 71
Computers for crime analysis	% of agencies using computers for analysis	Graph 72
Computers for dispatch	% of agencies using computers for dispatch	Graph 73
Computers for arrest	% of agencies using computers for arrest	Graph 74
In field CAD	% agencies with in field calls for service	Graph 75
Computers for warrants	% agencies using computers for warrants	Graph 76
Computers for traffic	% agencies using computers for traffic warrants	Graph 77
Computers for UCR	% agencies using for UCR file management	Graph 78
Computers for NIBRS	% agencies using for NIBRS file management	Graph 79
Personal computers	% agencies using personal computers	Graph 80
Mainframe	% agencies using mainframe computers	Graph 81

Variable	Construction	Appendix 1 Reference
Domestic violence policies	% with written policies regarding d.v.	Graph 82
Citizen complaint policies	% with written policies regarding complaints	Graph 83
Discretionary arrest	% with written policies on discretionary arrest	Graph 84
COPS	% with formal COPS program	Graph 85
Informal COPS	% with informal COPS program	Graph 86
Community meetings	% with community meetings	Graph 87
Problem solving	% engage in community problem solving	Graph 88
Citizen training	% offering citizen training	Graph 89
Field computers	% with in-field computers	Graph 90
Foot patrol	% agencies utilizing foot patrol	Graph 91
Bike patrol	% agencies utilizing bike patrol	Graph 92
Motorcycle patrol	% with motorcycle patrol	Graph 93
In field calls for service local agencies	% local agencies with in field capabilities	Graph 94
In field criminal history	% with in field capabilities	Graph 95
UCR/NIBRS		
UCR population coverage	agencies reporting 12 months divided by total population covered by UCR*100	Graph 22
NIBRS coverage	population covered by NIBRS divided by total US population*100	Graph 23
Arrest ratio	ratio of aggravated to simple assault arrests	Graph 24
Percent civilian	percentage of civilian employees in U.S. police departments	Graph 25
Percent commercial robbery	percent of UCR-recorded robberies that are commercial	Graph 26
UCR population base	denominator base used in UCR rates	Graph 27
Aggravated assault arrests	number of arrests derived from CIUS	Graph 28
Simple assault arrests	number of arrests derived from CIUS	Graph 29
Total agencies	total number of agencies reporting under the UCR, derived from CIUS	Graph 30
NIBRS states	number of states testing or certified to report under NIBRS format	Graph 31
NIBRS population	raw population count of persons covered under NIBRS	Graph 32

Variable	Construction	Appendix 1 Reference
Family offense arrests	number of annual arrests for family related offenses, derived from CIUS	Graph 33
Census		
White male	% U.S. population of white males	Graph 96
Male population	% population that is male	Graph 97
Female population	% population that is female	Graph 98
Males under 24	% population under 24 years of age	Graph 99
Black population	% of population that is black	Graph 100
Single	% of population that is single	Graph 101
Higher education	% with 4+ years of education	Graph 102
Living alone	% of population living alone	Graph 103
Prison population	% of population in prison	Graph 104
Jail population	% of population in jail	Graph 105
Hispanic	% of population that is Hispanic	Graph 106
English speaking	% that speak not well/not at all	Graph 107
No telephone	% population with no telephone	Graph 108
Homeowner move	% that have moved in last year	Graph 109
Renters move	% that have moved in last year	Graph 110
Homeowner live alone	% living alone	Graph 111
Renter live alone	% of population that live alone	Graph 112
GSS		
Not okay for police to hit male suspect	% approving	Graph 113
Okay for police to hit when attacked	% approving	Graph 114
Okay for police to hit escapee	% approving	Graph 115
Okay for police to hit for vulgar language	% approving	Graph 116
Okay for police to hit murder suspect	% approving	Graph 117
GSS: Afraid to walk alone at night in neighborhood	% responding yes	Graph 118
Gallup: Afraid to walk alone at night in neighborhood	% responding yes	Graph 119
Too little money spent on crime control	% responding yes	Graph 120
Courts are harsh enough with criminals	% responding yes	Graph 121
Police ethics are high	% responding yes	Graph 122

Variable	Construction	Appendix 1 Reference
Marijuana should be legalized	% responding yes	Graph 123
Laws against homosexuality	% responding yes	Graph 124
Wiretapping is okay	% approving	Graph 125
Confidence in police to protect	% responding yes	Graph 126
Domestic Violence Legislation		
Any protection from abuse legislation	% of U.S. population covered by legislation	Graph 127
No contact protection order	% of U.S. population covered by legislation	Graph 128
Eligibility beyond cohabitation	% of U.S. population covered by legislation	Graph 129
Victim custody relief	% of U.S. population covered by legislation	Graph 130
Misdemeanor for violating PO	% of U.S. population covered by legislation	Graph 131
Civil or criminal contempt for violations	% of U.S. population covered by legislation	Graph 132
Felony for violating PO	% of U.S. population covered by legislation	Graph 133
Warrantless arrest is okay	% of U.S. population covered by legislation	Graph 134
Mandatory arrest for PO violation	% of U.S. population covered by legislation	Graph 135
Firearm confiscation for PO violation	% of U.S. population covered by legislation	Graph 136

LEMAS

LEMAS data are used in a way that allows for the observation of whether organizational changes in policing are driving the increased correspondence. The LEMAS survey was first fielded in 1987 and covers over 3,000 state and local law enforcement agencies. The data provide a rich dataset with a wide range of information about law enforcement at the national level. The survey is administered every three years, 1990, 1993, 1997, 1999, and 2000. The sampling frame for the survey is generated through a multi-stage stratified sampling process. A listing of police departments is derived from the Directory of Survey of Law Enforcement Agencies. From this listing, police agencies are identified as either self-representing or not self-representing.

Self-representing agencies are those that employ 100 or more officers at the time of the survey. Agencies employing less than 100 officers at the time of interview are not self-representing. Self-representing agencies are sampled with certainty, and this means that they are sampled as representative of all agencies sharing their same characteristics. Agencies designated as not self-representing are randomly sampled and surveyed. The BJS produces parallel publications based on the LEMAS surveys. These two streams of LEMAS publications are generated based on estimates from the full sample and a subset of the sample.

The publication *Local Police Departments* is generated from the nationally representative sample including both representing and non-representing agencies. This publication presents estimates by size of the police agency and is derived from both sampling frames. Publications were released in 1987, 1990, 1993, 1997, and 2000. Prior to 1990, the publication included sheriff's departments as well; however, beginning in 1990 this publication reports on police departments only. The second stream of publications is based on all police departments that employ 100 or more officers at the time of the interview. This publication is titled *Law Enforcement Management and Administrative: Data for Individual States and Local Agencies with 100 or More Officers.* This publication provides a summary of all agencies as well as a breakdown of each reporting agency by state.

The present study assumes that the fuller sample is more representative of the broad organizational changes being tested. The major dimensions of police change can be effectively captured in this manner even though smaller agencies are sub-sampled across the years. Further, key variables of computerization, training, and recording practices are measured as percentages of the sampled responding police departments reporting affirmative to those items. Because imputation procedures and coverage will change between iterations of the survey, estimates generated by the BJS are utilized for the current research.

Though information from this data source is limited to the years 1987-2000, LEMAS can be used to augment the analysis through visual inspection and comparison of trends to other longitudinal variables. The benefit of these data is that they provide similarly gathered information on the police but from one centralized location. Additionally, the survey is a recent and more frequently utilized source of data on the police.

The surveys consist of various sections wherein agencies are asked questions regarding their usage of computers, the types of files maintained by computer (e.g. calls for services and field interviews), and the manner in which data are transmitted between the departments and field personnel. In addition, LEMAS queries enforcement agencies regarding their community policing programs, screening techniques, educational requirements, and training requirements for officers. Using these sources, a data series is generated to reflect changes in police professionalization, use of technology, and computerization (see also Langworthy 2002, 1999; Maguire 2002; Maguire, Snipes, Townsend, and Uchida 1998).

Variables for this data source are presented in Graphs 57-92 of Appendix 1 and are presented in the text of Table 5. One notable variable to be used in the analysis is the percentage of police departments participating in 911 emergency services (Graph 64). The construction of this variable merits discussion. A survey question asking about participation has been fielded in all iterations of the survey. Emergency telephone services bear directly on the research question at hand because any factor that facilitates the reporting of crime by victims to the police will influence greater correspondence between crimes captured by both series.

Since LEMAS information on this variable is only available going back to 1987, research on the origin of 911 emergency services was conducted. A search of the United States congressional record for May 27, 1999 revealed comments by the Representative of Alabama, Robert B. Aderholt, in which the origin of 911 is placed in Alabama during the year 1968. Assuming that in 1967, emergency participation was at 0 percent, a linear imputation method is used to create a time series for 911 participation over the course of this study. One limitation of this method is that 911 participation in police departments has not been linear over time and has most likely followed a growth curve pattern. This is the case especially during the 1970s. Additionally, organizational changes of this nature were occurring most rapidly in mid- to large-size police departments. Despite this shortcoming, this measure is the best that is available and is used in this study as a proxy for the true rate of 911participation during the study period. Due to the limited nature of the LEMAS data set, this source is sparingly used beyond the preliminary analysis.

Crime in the United States (CIUS)

Additional data on organizational change in policing was generated from CIUS. Previous researchers have noted that organizational changes in policing are reflected by the increased percent of the police workforce that is civilian (Biderman and Lynch, 1991; Walker, 1977). Civilian personnel are less likely to downgrade or screen out citizen complaints (Baker, Nienstedt, and Everett 1983; McCleary, Bienstadt, and Erven, 1982) thereby increasing the fraction of criminal events eligible to be recorded to the police (Biderman and Lynch, 1991). These data are readily available by year in the yearly UCR publication *Crime in the United States*, and will be used as an additional measure of changing police organizational structure.

Variables generated from CIUS include the ratio of aggravated to simple assault arrests, the population covered by UCR, the percentage of civilian employees in U.S. police departments, and the number of arrests for offenses against families and children. Table 5 presents variables constructed from the UCR for use in the present study and an accompanying reference for graphs of the variables in Appendix 1. A brief discussion of the general trends amongst these variables is now presented.

One frequently cited shortcoming of UCR-derived crime estimates is the unknown level of imputation used to generate estimates. Not all agencies submit complete crime counts during any given year. Though the actual number or percentage of agencies actually submitting full data during any given year is not readily available, an approximation may be generated from CIUS (Maltz, 1999). When agencies do not report for a specific time period, FBI analysts employ various imputation methods to estimate crime counts for missing data. These imputation methods have varied over time and with respect to different geographic units and are sometimes difficult to discern. However, two tables within CIUS provide information with which to calculate an approximate measure for populations covered by full reporting agencies.

Each year the FBI generates two tables for CIUS that present (1) estimates for all agencies, covering the entire U.S. population that have submitted data at any point during the year, and (2) counts for all agencies submitting a full twelve months of data. The actual table numbers vary across years but are generally titled *Index of Crime, United States* and *Rate: Number of Crimes per 100,000 Inhabitants*. Thus, for the former the population used in the denominator represents the entire U.S. population covered by the UCR while the latter represents only the population covered by agencies with complete reporting for the entire year (Nancy Carns, FBI, personal communication).

Dividing the population for agencies with full reporting by the population for which full and imputed counts are generated generates a coverage variable. This ratio is then multiplied by 100 to arrive at a percentage for the population covered. Graph 22 shows that actual coverage has varied between 81 and 91 percent for the period covered by this study, and coverage has steadily declined since approximately 1985. Because UCR coverage is frequently referenced as an important factor in the production of crime rates, it is included in the subsequent analysis.

Additional UCR-derived variables include the ratio of aggravated to simple assault. This variable is presented in Graph 24 and shows that over time police are recording increasingly more aggravated assault arrests than simple assault arrests. Previous research has hypothesized that as assaults are upgraded, more UCR-recorded levels of serious violent crime will increase as well. Visual inspection of this variable does indeed reflect that upgrading of simple assaults may be occurring for the crime category overall and that this may have a relationship to the seeming correspondence between UCR-recorded and NCVS-reported serious violent crime. The yearly of number of arrests for offenses against family and children is included in Graph 33. This variable shows a strong general upwards trend over time most likely similar to the upgrading dynamic associated with the ratio of aggravated to simple assault arrests.

Another factor conducive to the upgrading of crime incidence is the percentage of civilian employees working in police departments. Biderman and Lynch (1991) suggest that as the number of these employees increases, there is less discretion in the handling of crimes reported directly to law enforcement. CIUS reports the annual percentage of civilian employees and this variable was taken directly from the annual reports. Graph 25 presents this variable, and though the upward trend is marginal at best, there is a generally increasing trend over time of the percentage of civilian employees in the nation's police departments.

The percentage of commercial robberies is another variable generated from CIUS and included in the current study. The FBI includes commercial robberies within its crime counts while the NCVS does not. This raises issues of comparability between the two series. A variable is generated from CIUS to control for this definitional difference between the two series. This variable is presented in Graph 26 of Appendix 1. Though there has been variation in the percentage of commercial robberies over time, the general trend of this variable appears relatively stable and fluctuates between 20 and 24 percent. The influence of this variable on the seeming correspondence appears minimal from the visual inspection; however, it is retained for the analyses due to the strong methodological implications cited in previous research (Biderman and Lynch, 1991). For the interested reader, Appendix 1 provides graphs of additional variables that were used to construct included variables. These remain in the appendix but are not discussed further in the text.

NIBRS

Whereas data collected under the UCR program are released annually as *Crime in the United States*, to date no comparable annual publication based on NIBRS data exists (Jeanine Arnold, FBI personal communication). For those states and agencies collecting crime data under the NIBRS format, the FBI converts all the data into the summary format of the UCR prior to compiling estimates for the yearly CIUS bulletin.

Additionally, there are very few historical or archival data that capture yearly changes in either the percentage of state populations covered by the NIBRS or the number of states certified by year (Greg Swanson, FBI personal communication). For the present study, an ideal measure of yearly NIBRS change would be the yearly percentage of the national population covered by NIBRS.

Two methods were used to generate a population coverage variable for NIBRS. The first was to use a BJS sponsored publication that presents the total population covered by NIBRS for the years 1990-1994. The second was to directly access NIBRS data files from the Inter-university Consortium for Political and Social Research and extract the number of agencies reporting under the NIBRS format and their associated populations. Using the above two sources a numerator for NIBRS was generated and a UCR-derived denominator for the total U.S. population was used to arrive at a ratio for NIBRS coverage to total UCR population. This ratio was then multiplied by 100 to arrive at a percentage of the population covered by NIBRS annually. The NIBRS coverage variable represents agencies reporting for a full 12 months under the NIBRS format and is presented in Graph 23 of Appendix 1. The variable shows a strong upward trend over time.

As of 2002, only 24 states have been NIBRS certified by the FBI (Greg Swanson, FBI personal communication). For the year 2002, these states represent 17 percent of the current U.S. population, approximately 15 percent of reported crime in the United States, and 25 percent of law enforcement agencies (Swanson, 2003). Certification means that each state has proven its ability to gather and report crime under the NIBRS format, and more importantly, that the FBI accepts NIBRS data from either the state or qualifying state agencies. For states that are certified the Status Report lists the name of the state and the start date for the testing of NIBRS. Additionally, for certified states, year 2002 data are reported for the number of NIBRS agencies, the percentage of state population represented by NIBRS, and the percentage of state crime reported through NIBRS.

For states in the testing phase, the NIBRS Status Report provides the date that NIBRS testing began for each respective state. The testing phase indicates that preliminary test data from various agencies within the state are submitted to the FBI. However, no other information, such as number of agencies, is available for states in the testing stage. States in the developmental stage of NIBRS are in the process of design and implementation of protocols associated with NIBRS data collection. Ten states fit this description and are listed in the developmental stage. Lastly, six states are listed as having no formalized plan to transition to NIBRS, indicating that the state either has no interest in transitioning to NIBRS or does not have a formalized plan.

The nature of this study does not require a precise measure of NIBRS participation for two reasons. First, given that crime data in this format are converted to summary format and included in the UCR estimates, there is no expectation that the NIBRS will be "siphoning off" police-recorded crimes from the UCR. Second, hypothesis number four suggests that the design, testing, and implementation of NIBRS itself will not facilitate greater recording but that it may create greater awareness for recording protocols among various agencies within states and across the larger law enforcement community.

Regardless, the explanatory variable for NIBRS is used herein as a proxy for organizational change and innovation in agencies across the United States (see Rantala, 2000 for additional discussion of the effect of NIBRS on crime statistics).

DEMOGRAPHIC VARIABLES

Data from the United States Bureau of the Census are used to measure changes in the demographic composition of the population. The Census is conducted every ten years with inter-censal estimates available during interim years for many variables except for demographic composition variables related to sex, race, and ethnicity, living arrangements, mobility, and a variety of other population characteristics. The Census gathers information in two formats: a short form administered to every person and household, and a long form which is administered to a random sample of persons.

For research purposes, national population estimates are usually generated from the long form Census questionnaire that is administered to every individual during the decennial survey. Sample estimates are generated from short form surveys that are administered to a random subset of the national population. As such, these estimates are subject to both sampling and non-sampling error. In both cases inter-censal estimates can be generated; however, depending on the variable in question the nature of the estimates is slightly different. Some inter-censal estimates are based on population counts while other inter-censal estimates are based on survey population data.

Additionally, the availability of these estimates is not necessarily consistent across the period covered by this study. The implications of this are discussed below. Hence for the present study demographic composition variables are derived from a different source than population characteristic variables derived from samples such as the percentage of the population living alone and the percentage of the population moving within the last year.

The second format is a long form administered randomly to a representative sample of the population such that approximately one in every six persons and households is surveyed. From individuals, the long form solicits more detailed information regarding marital status, educational attainment, labor force status, language spoken at home and ability to speak English (ability to communicate with police), and income. With regard to household, the long form solicits information on mobility, telephone service, and value of the residence. Measures to be used from the census will include ability to communicate in English, education, living arrangements, and mobility.

Demographic Composition—Age, Sex, Race, and Ethnicity

This study uses four major demographic variables: age, sex, race, and ethnicity. Each of these variables has a different story with regards to available estimates covering the study time period 1970-2002. Due to definitional ambiguities, the issue of race and ethnicity is still under review by the Bureau of the Census. Primarily there is lack of consensus on how best to put measures of race and ethnicity together. The Bureau of the Census has inter-censal estimates of racial composition for the years 1990-2002 broken down by the classifications of white and black. Other groupings have changed markedly over the years, leaving only crude measures as indicators of racial population composition. These estimates are available electronically through their website; however, prior to 1990 there are neither population nor sample inter-censal estimates for racial composition (George Spencer, Bureau of the Census personal communication).

The case of ethnicity provides an example of changing procedures related to the Population Census. Questions regarding ethnicity, specifically Hispanic origin, were asked of sample populations beginning in 1970. Beginning with the 1980 Census, questions regarding Hispanic origin were asked of all surveyed individuals, i.e., the entire population. While data based on population and sample data are available, merging estimates across these years is problematic. Prior to 1980 estimates are susceptible to an unknown quantity of sampling error that is not present in post-1980 estimates. Thus, officially the Census Bureau does not have this type of data available publicly.

However, in the early 1990s the National Center for Health Statistics (NCHS) commissioned the Bureau of the Census to generate race and ethnicity estimates for interim years of the Population Survey. The NCHS desired to show meaningful relationships for death rates across racial and ethnic groups. Hence, although the Bureau of the Census does not produce these estimates for public use and access through their publications or website, the data are available as the denominator in NCHS rates of mortality. NCHS was contacted directly. Though historical data are not available through their website (www.cdc.gov/nchs), a request was presented to gain access to the data used to compute the denominators of their variables. Therefore measures on demographic composition for this study do not come directly from population estimates available from the Bureau of the Census. Instead, they are derived from bridged race estimates generated by the Bureau of the Census under a special request for the National Center for Health Statistics.

There are two available sources of unpublished bridged estimates. A PDF file with years 1960-1997 is available broken down by race, age, and sex. In this document race is broken down into black and white categories. The file is disaggregated into ten-year age ranges for white males, black males, white females, and black females; however, national totals are available as well. The file was created prior to the 2000 Census, meaning that inter-censal estimates of racial composition for the 1990s are based solely on the 1990 Census and do not incorporate the 2000 Census (Brady Hamilton, NCHS personal communication).

In contrast, estimates for the 1980s-, do incorporate results from the 1990 Census and are thus more precise and valid. The second source of data from the NCHS is the actual bridged race estimates for years 1990-2001. For estimates extending from 1990-1999, both year 1990 and 2000 decennial censuses are used. The estimates for year 2001 and 2002 are based solely on the year 2000 Census. These files are easily accessible in ASCII format that may be read into any widely used statistical package. The raw data file contains all race, age, and sex groupings by both state and county. Though there are no national tallies available for each year, computing the population for each racial category is a simple process of aggregating and summing across the groups.

In computing the estimates the NCHS counts are set up against the categories provided by the Census (Brady Hamilton, NCHS personal communication). For the present study, these estimates were used rather than the interpolation method of subtracting on decennial population from a previous count and then dividing the difference through by the years in between. All demographic composition variables related to age, race, sex, and ethnicity are presented in Appendix 1, Graphs 96-106.

Education

The Bureau of the Census does not have estimates for education based on population counts prior to 1990; however, sample estimates for education do exist for the years 1972-2002. When using sample estimates it is better to use percentages rather than exact counts that can be influenced by sampling error because a percentage will capture the distribution of the variable across the population. Unfortunately percentage distributions for education are not available going back to 1970, even for sample estimates.

Rather than splice pre-and post-1990 estimates based on divergent population estimates (i.e. national and sample populations), this study uses the raw count numbers made available through the Department of the Census' website in conjunction with total population estimates to create percentages. Though the counts are prone to sampling error and have a tendency to "bounce around" (George Spencer, Bureau of the Census personal communication) they provide the best consistent measure of this variable over time. Additionally, because this study focuses on large-scale national trends rather than precise cross-sectional parameter estimates, instability and slight variations in the standard error associated with raw counts is less problematic.

Population Characteristics

As with education, the remainder of Census related variables used in this study are derived from short-form sample questionnaires. These variables are chosen because previous research suggests that factors such as mobility, living arrangements, and ability to contact law enforcement may be related to a victim's report of criminal victimization being recorded by law enforcement (Biderman and Lynch, 1991; Hindelang, Gottfredson, and Garafolo, 1978).

The variables include additional factors such as percentage of the population with a telephone, percentage of the population that are renters or homeowners, mobility (whether homeowners and renters have moved within the last year), the percentage of the population living alone, and the percentage of the population that is single. Two additional variables are included to capture high-risk populations that may not be captured in NCVS crime counts. Though these variables are not Census derived they are included in this section due to their relationship to overall population characteristics. These variables are the percentage of the population in prison and jail and were derived from historical and contemporary BJS documents (Calahan, 1986).

These variables are listed textually in Table 5 and are presented graphically as Figures 96-112 in Appendix 1. For the most part Census related variables examined in this study do not show a strong upward trend that may be related to the seeming congruence between police-recorded and victim-reported violent crime. Variables showing virtually no relationship include: population percentages of white males, females, males under twenty-four years of age, blacks, single unmarried persons, persons living alone, persons not speaking English well, and mobility within the last year for both renters and homeowners.

Variables showing some upward trend over time include percentages of the population with four or more years of college education, in prison, that are Hispanic, and homeowners that live alone. Additionally, the decline in persons without a telephone appears inversely related (from visual inspection) to the increasing correspondence. This is not surprising since having a telephone allows a crime victim or witness to more readily contact authorities.

SOCIAL ATTITUDES

Data on changing social perceptions regarding crime are generated from the General Social Survey (GSS) and from data on domestic violence graciously extended to the author by Laura Dugan. Each of these data sources is discussed below.

GSS

The GSS is conducted by the National Opinion Research Center, and aside from the years 1979 and 1981, the survey was conducted yearly from 1972 to 1993. Beginning in 1994, the survey has been conducted bi-annually. The survey measures public attitudes toward various social issues and frequently incorporates contemporary issues into the survey questions. Social concerns on topical issues such as freedom, religion, and the feminization of poverty are examined in various years. Questionnaire items and wording are constructed in to facilitate time trend studies, making the GSS a useful dataset for assessing long-term changes in public perceptions. The survey is administered to a stratified multi-stage probability sample drawn from the non-institutionalized English speaking population who are 18 years and older in the United States.

The ideal measure for this study is one that captures the correlation between public and police attitudes toward crime and violence over time. If an increase in the correlation between these two indicators were present across time, this would be supportive of the hypothesis that greater agreement toward definitions of crime was occurring. Unfortunately such a measure does not exist. However, several related measures do and will be explored as proxies to capture these underlying social processes.

For example, several survey items measure public sentiment toward the police, violence, and crime. Three categories of questions ask respondents for their feelings toward the police and enforcement activities. From 1972-1998 respondents were asked whether it was acceptable for an officer to strike a suspect under a variety of scenarios. Between 1983-1991 several questions were fielded to respondents regarding their feelings toward police use of surveillance.

These responses will be used to measure change in public sentiment toward use of police power. Presumably if public perceptions toward and willingness to engage the police have changed over time, this might be reflected in public sentiment toward the use of police power. The last measure of changing perceptions toward enforcement personnel will be measured by an item that was fielded from 1983-1987, 1988-1991, and again in 1996. This item asks respondents whether they felt that more money should be spent on law enforcement and the police.

Several survey items measure changing public sentiment regarding violence and feelings toward crime. Between 1972 and 1994 a battery of questions asked respondents to reflect on whether they would approve of a man punching another man under certain situations. These measures are used to determine whether there has been a change in public perceptions of violence. Another source of changing public sentiment available through the GSS is a series of questions fielded between 1972-1998 in which respondents were asked whether they felt that too much money was being spent on halting the rising crime rate. If greater agreement between the public and police is present over time this may result in less variance over time in survey items tapping into these processes.

Additionally a question regarding the respondent's feelings toward court severity has been asked of survey respondents. The question was first fielded in 1973, at which time 66 percent of respondents felt that the courts did not deal harshly enough with criminals. By 1985, 85 percent of respondents felt that the courts did not deal harshly enough with criminals. However, by year 2000 the percentage of respondents who felt that courts were too lenient with criminals had nearly returned to 1973 levels, with 68 percent of respondents stating they felt courts were not harsh enough.

This may indicate that more people are comfortable with the criminal justice system and, by extension, law enforcement. General attitudinal feelings regarding feelings of safety, confidence in the ability of the police to protect the public, and feelings regarding the ethics of law enforcement are included as well. Two questions are utilized to tap into public perceptions regarding deviancy and changing perceptions of socially acceptable behavior: support for the legalization of marihuana and support for laws against homosexual relationships. Though these measures are crude, they are the only ones available through GSS that tap into the underlying construct of attitudes regarding deviancy.

Graphs 140-153 in Appendix 1 present all GSS-related variables examined for this study. There has been a general decline in public support for police violence toward the public (shown in Graphs 113-116), although in recent years a slight upward movement in the trend line is present in public support for a police officer striking a murder suspect (Figure 117). However, there are too few time points to discern whether this is a true upward trend.

There has been a steady decline in the percentage of respondents stating they are afraid to walk alone in their neighborhoods at night. This is true whether measured by GSS or the Gallup Poll (Graphs 118 and 119). This possibly reflects a greater confidence in police ability to protect. Indeed, Graph 126 (confidence in ability of police to protect) shows a marked increase over time. Likewise, Figure 122 shows there has been an increase in the percentage of respondents stating that the ethics of the police are very high or high. Views of deviancy or tolerance of socially diverse behaviors have changed as well over time. The percentage of respondents stating they approve of the legalization of marihuana has increased over time, while the percentage in favor of legislation against homosexual relationships has declined during the study period.

Domestic Violence

Over the past 30 years probably no change in social perceptions has been as dramatic as perceptions regarding domestic violence. Quality data on domestic violence at the national level are either difficult to obtain or nonexistent, especially for a longitudinal study such as this one. The ideal measure for changes in domestic violence would be a survey question asking respondents their views on this as a crime over time. No such measure exists. However, the passing of legislation and changes in the criminal treatment of offenders for this crime may be seen as a proxy for a survey-based question that taps into public support for increased harshness when dealing with offenders.

Data related to legislation on domestic violence are derived from a previous study that examined changes in state-level legislation for the years 1976-1997 (Dugan, Nagin, and Rosenfeld, 2003). Though originally intended for state-level analysis, these data were easily aggregated to a national level and a percentage was generated to reflect the percentage of the U.S. population that is covered by certain types of domestic violence legislation.

These variables are presented in Graphs 127-136 of Appendix 1. With one exception, felony protection for a protection order violation (Graph 133), all of these measures show a significant upward trend over time. The variables are more fully discussed in Table 5. However, the variables capture elements of state legislation such as victim advocacy (e.g., victim custody relief and eligibility beyond cohabitation), arrest procedures (e.g., warrantless and mandatory arrest), and penal responses (e.g., felony and misdemeanor charges for violations, civil and criminal contempt, and firearm confiscation for violations). Due to the nature of domestic violence, these measures are most likely associated with changes in the handling of assault cases, and more specifically as it pertains to this study, the crime of aggravated assault. Changes in state legislation are reflective of broader social responses to a specific crime, and as such are a valid proxy for public sentiment toward violence against women and children.

DESIGN CHANGES

Both the UCR and NCVS have undergone design changes. However, as suggested by Biderman and Lynch (1991) within-series variation may likewise introduce intra-series variation over time. The effects of such change can be explored by the introduction of control variables. Series-specific control variables are generated to examine their influence on changes in the UCR and NCVS organization and methodology. By far there is greater information regarding changes to the NCVS, with little information regarding internal changes (e.g., imputation methods) for the UCR. In light of this the following discussion will briefly discuss easily identifiable changes to both programs but the interested reader is may consult Appendix 2 for a more detailed accounting of changes to the NCVS over time.

NCVS Design Changes

Data on NCVS design changes was generated from the methodology sections of the yearly *Criminal Victimization in the United States* for the years 1973-1996 and from the online Statistical Tables publicly available through the BJS publications website (http://www.ojp.usdoj. gov/bjs/pubalp2.htm). Over the years several changes in design and implementation have occurred. Additionally, there has been a change in how published estimates are generated from the survey. Appendix 2 chronologically presents many of the NCVS design changes highlighted in the methodology sections of the yearly bulletins. The second change affects the publication of national victimization estimates generated by the survey data. This is discussed more fully below.

A longstanding concern with NCVS victimization estimates is that due to the retrospective nature of the survey, collection of data for victimizations during a specific year will not be available until surveys have been administered for the month of June during the following year. However, within the past decade the BJS has modified the manner in which estimates are generated such that national level estimates are more readily available.

Prior to 1996, victimization estimates were generated based on data-year data. Data year, as the name implies, simply means that the estimates produced were computed from information on surveys that pertain to a specific year. An example will illustrate. As mentioned previously, the NCVS survey is administered monthly to a rotating sample. Respondents are asked to report on victimizations they have experienced within the past six months. Hence a respondent surveyed during the month of June in one year may very well report a victimization that occurred during the month of December the previous year. Preparation of the data and subsequent analyses push the release date of estimates back even further. Between 1973 and 1995, yearly bulletins published by the BJS using data year were titled Criminal Victimization in the United States. Beginning in 1996, yearly estimates using data year are only available online electronically as Criminal Victimization in the United States, Statistical Tables.

An alternative approach is to publish national estimates based upon collection year data. Though not as intuitively understood as data year, collection year data simply means that victimization estimates are based upon all data collected from interviews administered during any given year. Returning to the example above, victimization estimates would be based on all interviews completed within a given year. Rather than wait until June to capture possibly reported December victimizations, estimates are generated solely on the data gathered from surveys between January and December of the year in question. BJS reports utilizing collection year data are titled Criminal Victimization, Changes with Trends.

One benefit of using collection year data is related to timing. Since estimates are generated from interviews ending in December, national estimates of victimization are available around the same time CIUS is released by the FBI. Though changes to this protocol were first mentioned by the National Science Foundation evaluation (Penick and Owens 1976), it was not until recently that the changes were actually implemented. Starting in 1996 the BJS has generated reports based on collection year. Prior to implementation an evaluation examined whether resulting estimates were significantly different when based on data versus collection year. The differences between the generated estimates were not significantly different. In summary, there are currently two streams of publications produced by the BJS, Criminal Victimization in the United States and Criminal Victimization, Changes with Trends.

With respect to the current study, variables related to design change are taken together from two sources. For the years 1973-1995 design-related variables were taken from the methodology sections of the yearly Criminal Victimization in the United States bulletins. For the years 1996-2002 design-related variables were taken from the methodology sections of Criminal Victimization in the United States, Statistical Tables. Thus, for purposes of this study variables were extracted with respect to data year.

Though the NCVS redesign was implemented in 1992, several methodological changes occurring during the course of the survey are examined for this study. For instance, due to fiscal constraints an increasing percentage of telephone rather than in-person interviews have been conducted over the years. A control variable is generated to capture the annual percentage of planned phone interviews that have increased from 20 to 80 percent over the past twenty-nine years. Similarly, the percentage of computer-assisted telephone interviews is used as an explanatory variable in this study. These variables are presented in Graphs 36 and 37 of Appendix 1.

Additional procedural changes may produce inter-series variation over time. Biderman and Lynch (1991) suggest that during economic upturns, mobility among the population increases. The result is an increase in the number of unbounded NCVS interviews in the sample that can affect victimization estimates over time. The annual number of unbounded interviews (Graph 41) is discerned from the NCVS data file and a variable generated to control for these effects. Other control variables include measures to capture the annual person response rate (Graph 35), the annual sample size (Graph 50), and dummy variables to for pre-and post-redesign years of the NCVS (Graph 40), change in proxy interviews (Graph 39), and the reduction in the primary sampling units that occurred in 1985 (Graph 38).

Of concern to both BJS and the Census Department, person response rate has declined over time. The NCVS still retains the highest response rate of any government survey, but fewer persons responding to the survey has implications for victimization estimates, especially for rarer crimes such as rape and robbery (Atrostic, Bates, Burt, and Silberstein, 2001; Groves and Couper, 1998). The person response rate for the NCVS has declined in the last ten years from approximately 99 percent to 94 percent. Similarly Graph 51 of Appendix 1 shows that a decline has also occurred in the household response rate, although this has not been as dramatic as the decline in person response rate.

Because this study focuses on serious violent victimizations against individuals, lower person response rates may contribute to an underestimate of victimizations against potentially high risk persons who are more infrequently at home. Thus, a declining person response rate may mean that violent victimizations most likely to be reported to the police will show up in official records but not necessarily NCVS victimization counts.

Graphs 42-45 of Appendix 1 present the percentage of series victimizations that are included in national victimization estimates. Some research suggests that the influence of series crimes may be variable over time and hence influence national estimates (Planty, 2004). A series crime is defined as a number of incidents that are so similar in nature that the victim is unable to distinguish the details of each incident separately (Dodge, 1987). Series crimes present a problem for victimization estimates because the appropriate counting mechanism for including them in estimates is ambiguous.

Prior to 1992 series crimes were defined as three or more such events, yet following the redesign the minimum number of incidents to qualify as a series crime was raised from three to six because research indicated that with proper interviewer prompts respondents were able to distinguish up to six similar events. Additionally, during the earlier years of the survey the reference period for reporting series crimes was slightly different than the reference period for other victimizations. In later years of the survey, however, recall of cues for series crimes was modified to include the same six-month reference period as for other victimizations. The effect of this change on aggregate counts is questionable, though as Dodge (1987) reports that in prior years there was an 87.5 percent overlap between the time period covered by series victimizations versus other victimizations.

A series crime implies that an incident may have occurred six or more times, so it is unclear whether to count these victimizations as occurring once, twice, three times, or some average of the number of series crimes reported by the victim. Series crimes are excluded from annual victimization estimates but are included in special reports such as those investigating intimate partner violence. The current project uses NCVS estimates that exclude series crimes but examines the possible influence of varying levels of series victimization over time.

For the most part the influence of these variables is negligible, as presented in Graphs 42-45 of Appendix 1. For instance, Graph 43 shows that rapes defined as series crimes have fluctuated between 2.5 and 9.9 percent of total rape victimizations reported to interviewers.

Lastly, Graphs 52-56 show the percentage of violent crimes reported to the police as measured by the NCVS. These graphs are provided for illustrative purposes only. With the exception of aggravated assault, reporting rates for all crime types has been increasing. The fact that aggravated assault is the only crime not being reported at higher levels lends support to the notion that the congruence in this crime category may be motivated more by police response.

UCR Design Changes

Discerning design-related change from the UCR is a far more difficult task. There is no historical documentation as with the NCVS and as such researchers in the past have made due with what little information may be distinguished from published documents (Biderman and Lynch, 1991; Maltz, 1999). For the purpose of this study the following variables were generated as proxies for methodological and organizational change to the UCR. Due to their dual relevance in other sections they have been briefly discussed before: the percentage of the population covered by UCR agencies reporting for a full twelve months, the ratio of aggravated to simple assaults, the percentage of the population covered under NIBRS, and the percentage of the workforce that is civilian.

These variables are presented in Appendix 1 in Graphs 22-25, respectively. Graphs 28 and 29 present the number of aggravated and simple assault arrests over time. These two variables were used to generate the arrest ratio, and from a visual inspection of these two components it is evident that while simple assault arrests have steadily increased, the number of aggravated assault arrests has grown at a greater pace.

CHAPTER 5

Hypotheses and Analysis

Increasingly more criminal justice related data are available for trend analysis of crime and justice. Though the UCR has been underway since 1933, the NCVS is only now entering its thirtieth year of data collection. With three decades of crime data now available for research, examination of long-term crime trends is finally becoming possible. Additionally for many years researchers attempted to explain why victim reporting and police-recorded crime totals differ, so the recent convergence allows an opportunity to further examine the influence of variables related to four possible explanations.

HYPOTHESES

Four research questions and related hypotheses guide the proposed research. The expectations of each hypothesis are discussed in greater detail below.

Changes in Policing

The first hypothesis is that the convergence between reported victimizations and police-recorded crime is positively related to changes in policing such as the implementation of technology, the increasing use of computerization, and changes in organization structure. For purposes of the present study, changes in policing is operationalized as administrative or organizational change that in turn influences functions within police departments. Changes of this nature include the percentage of civilians in the law enforcement workforce, the ratio of aggravated to simple assault arrests, the change from a uniform crime reporting system to an incident-based reporting system, and the percentage of police departments utilizing emergency-based 911 systems. Technology and computerization is measured by the increased presence of information systems such as personal computers for in-field service calls and the use of computers for information and data management such as warrants, records, arrests, and criminal investigation.

These changes to police administration, structure, and operation affect how the police go about their work. In some cases, for example the prevalence of 911, the changes mediate the ability of citizens to contact the police when a crime occurs. Other variables such as the arrest ratio and the transition to NIBRS function as indicators of police administrative changes. The ratio of aggravated to simple assault arrests will change over time if a general upgrading of assault cases has occurred. The theoretical expectation is that these factors will be positively associated with the convergence between victim reporting and police recording over time.

Hypothesis 1: The convergence is positively related to changes in policing such as the implementation of technology and computerization, changes in recording and administrative practices, and the ability of the citizenry to contact the police if they do experience a criminal victimization.

Changes in Population Characteristics

The reporting and recording of crime incidents may be influenced by demographic characteristics of the population. Certain population characteristics (e.g. sex, age, race, and education) are associated with the likelihood that victims will report crime. Likewise, police response to an incident may be influenced by the characteristics of those who report victimizations. For example, an older victim may be perceived as more legitimate than a younger victim may. A related hypothesis is that changes in the population composition have affected both the victim pool and offender pool in such a way as to contribute to an increasing number of crimes being reported to or recorded by the police. As the pool of potential victims increases in age or changes by sex or racial composition, the extent to which the population is willing to contact the police might change as well. Additionally officer discretion in the handling of criminal events may likewise be affected. If older persons are more likely to report being victimized, the extent to which the population has aged may be related to the overall level of police recording of eligible crime events.

Hypothesis 2: Fluctuations in the population of certain groups such as young males, the number of recent movers, persons with higher educational attainment, and the percentage of households without telephones affect both the victim and offender pool that contributes to an increase in the number of crimes being reported and recorded by police.

Social Changes in the Perception of Crime

Certain crimes have traditionally been less likely to be both reported by victims and recorded by police. Beginning in the 1970s and throughout the following decade, increasing attention was directed toward crimes such as domestic violence, rape, and assault. These crimes were traditionally underreported due to several factors, including the nature of the victim and offender relationship and the stigma attached to being a victim of these crimes.

However public and official perception of these crimes has changed over time and is evidenced in two ways. First, officers are in many instances now mandated to act in situations, such as those relating to domestic violence and rape, regardless of the victim offender relationship. Second, victim advocacy and resources for victims of crime are now generally accepted as a component in the criminal justice process. These types of changes will likely influence the behavior of officers and victims of these crimes. Victim assistance in the form of legal advocacy, crisis counseling and intervention, and domestic violence shelters has increased dramatically over the last thirty years. It seems unlikely that these broad based social changes have not influenced victim perceptions of crime and their willingness to seek assistance from police officers and others.

The third hypothesis of the current research is that perceptions of crime, violence, and the criminal justice system have changed over time. Hence a broader social agreement regarding definitions of crime, feelings toward violence, and the ability of the criminal justice system to respond to crimes now exists. In addition, when victimized individuals contact the police, the police are increasingly willing to respond formally to victim reports of crime. This in turn creates a paper record where one would not have existed prior.

Variables capturing perceptions of the police are derived from the GSS. Several questions ask respondents about perceptions of law enforcement and the criminal justice system more generally. Variables related to domestic violence legislation are included as a proxy for broader based awareness regarding violence toward women. If social attitudes are broadly based, these variables will be positively related to the correspondence between reporting and recording over time. Variables examined with respect to this hypothesis include perceptions of the court system, ethics of the police, confidence in the role of the police as protectors, violence on the part of the police, and the percentage of the U.S. population covered by certain types of domestic violence legislation. The theoretical expectation is that the correspondence will be conditioned by changes in public support for the police and perceptions of crimes and violence over time.

Hypothesis 3: Perceptions of crime, violence, and support of the criminal justice system have changed over time such that there is now greater agreement regarding definitions and response to crime.

Methodological Design Changes

There is reason to believe that methodological changes in the implementation and administration of the NCVS and UCR will affect the correspondence between the two series. If series-specific redesigns have influenced the reporting and recording convergence, these effects should be empirically observable following the introduction of controls for competing explanatory variables. Originally this hypothesis included design changes related to the UCR. Throughout the research process, however, it became evident that changes to the UCR are not readily accessible. The effects of design change to the UCR are not known but should be acknowledged as contributing in some unknown fashion and quantity to changes in the series. For the purpose of this study, design-related changes focus on those related to the NCVS since this is the only collection program that provides a transparent accounting of design-related changes over time.

Hypothesis 4: The convergence is an artifact of methodological design change in the NCVS.

ANALYTIC STRATEGY

The research question and nature of the data creates unexpected issues to be resolved. First, the research question is a complicated topic that requires the collection of many explanatory variables. Second, the number of years for analysis is short. The remainder of this chapter presents a strategy for dealing with these two issues and the results of the analysis.

The analysis proceeds in two stages. The first stage includes examinations of the graphical presentations of the variables contained in Appendix 1 to ascertain whether increases similar to that evident in the correspondence are visible. Following visual inspection of the variables, descriptive statistics are discussed. The second stage of the analysis begins with multivariate analysis to determine best fitting models for each crime type. Any significant relationships identified in these models are graphed over time and modeled once but with the decomposed dependent variables to assess whether previously identified relationships affect one series more than the other series.

STAGE ONE ANALYSIS

Visual Inspection

Following visual inspection of the graphs in Appendix 1 it became evident that the aggregate measures for serious violent crime masked much of the crime-specific changes over time. The remainder of this study examines only the specific crime categories of rape, robbery, and aggravated assault. As presented in Appendix 1, several variations of the dependent variable were considered. Following preliminary analyses and for ease of presentation and interpretation, I use the dependent variable constructed as the number of UCR-recorded crimes divided by the number of NCVS-reported crimes. This ratio is then multiplied by 100 to generate a comparative rate of crime recorded between the NCVS and UCR.

Theoretically the dependent variable may range from 0 percent, if the police recorded no victimizations reported to them, to more than 100 percent if the police recorded more crimes than victims state they reported to police. The latter may have happened due to counting and definitional differences between the two series. Additionally, the dependent variable is not a measure of the percentage of total crime that the police can record but the ratio of victim-reported crime captured in police records. If the dependent variable was intended to capture a measure of total crime, it follows that the range of the dependent variable would be confined between 0 and 100 percent. However, in the case of the latter the dependent variable is a reflection of police-recorded crime as a percentage of victim-reported crime and may include values above 100 percent.

Explanatory variables are chosen with similar criteria. Any variable affecting the convergence requires that contributing factors must show changes over time if they are to be considered potential reasons for the correspondence. The graphs of variables presented in Appendix 1 are examined as potential influences, and any variable clearly showing notable change over time is identified as a possible contributor to increased correspondence.

Using this criterion, several variables are omitted from further consideration. In the cases of the second hypothesis, no relevant variables exhibited adequate variation to account for the correspondence in part or whole. This hypothesis is dropped from further consideration. Additional variables not meeting the minimum standard included NCVS design-related variables such as the percentage of unbounded interviews and the percentage of series crimes omitted from crime specific counts. This parsing of variables resulted in three remaining dependent variables and 34 explanatory variables to be examined in the first stage of the analysis. These variables and a brief description of them and their associated hypotheses are presented in Table 6.

Table 6. Variables and associated hypotheses used in the first stage of analysis

Variable	Description
Dependent Variables	
Rape	(UCR-recorded/NCVS-reported)×100
Robbery	(UCR-recorded/NCVS-reported)×100
Aggravated Assault	(UCR-recorded/NCVS-reported)×100
Independent Variables	
Year	Year scaled 1-29
Hypothesis 1: Police organization	
UCR Coverage	Percentage of police agencies reporting to UCR for full 12 months
NIBRS	Percentage of police agencies reporting under NIBRS format for full 12 months
Arrest ratio	Ratio of aggravated to simple assault arrests
% 911	Percentage of police agencies utilizing 911
% civilian	Percent civilian employees in police agencies
LEMAS in field	Percentage police agencies using computers for in field calls for service
LEMAS record keeping	Percentage police agencies using computers for record keeping
LEMAS criminal invest.	Percentage police agencies using computers for criminal investigation

Variable	Description
LEMAS arrest	Percentage police agencies using computers for arrest
LEMAS warrants	Percentage police agencies using computers for processing warrants
LEMAS personal	Percentage police agencies using personal computers
Hypothesis 2: Changes in social attitudes	
Police ethics	Percent of GSS respondents stating police ethics are very high/high
Confidence in police	Percent of GSS respondents stating they have confidence in the police to protect them
Not okay to strike	Percent of GSS respondents stating they can imagine a situation where an officer may strike a citizen
Courts harsh enough	Percent of GSS respondents stating that the criminal courts are harsh enough
Beyond cohabitation	Percentage of U.S. population covered by domestic violence protections beyond cohabitation
Warrantless arrest	Percentage of U.S. population covered by warrantless arrest for domestic violence
No contact PO	Percentage of U.S. population covered by no contact protection orders
Custody relief	Percentage of U.S. population covered by victim custody relief
Misdemeanor PO violation	Percentage of U.S. population covered by misdemeanor penalties for violation of protection orders
Civil/criminal penalty	Percentage of U.S. population covered by either civil or criminal contempt for domestic violence cases
Felony PO violation	Percentage of U.S. population covered by felony penalty for violation of protection order
Mandatory arrest	Percentage of U.S. population covered by mandatory arrest policies for violation of protection order
Firearm confiscation	Percentage of U.S. population covered by confiscation of firearms for violating protection order
Hypothesis 3: Changes in NCVS design	
Proxy interviews	Change in proxy interviews of respondents 12 years old. Dummy variable (0=13 and older; 1=12 and older)
Primary sampling unit reduction	Reduction in primary sampling units. Dummy variable (0=pre-reduction; 1=post-reduction)
Redesign	Dummy variable (0=pre-redesign; 1=post-redesign)
Person response	persons responding to the survey
CATI	Percentage of NCVS CATI interviews
Percent telephone	Percentage of NCVS telephone interviews

Descriptive Statistics

Table 7 presents descriptive statistics for the 34 variables. In looking at the dependent variables (i.e. rape, robbery, and aggravated assault) wide variation across the different offenses is apparent. In Figure 2 of the introduction we see that the reporting of serious violent crime fluctuates between 50and 60 percent between 1973 and 2002. However, when overall reporting to police is disaggregated by crime type (as presented in Table 7) greater variation is evident across the three categories. When examining the means for each crime type, the level of reporting is within 10 percentage points, but the ranges in reporting vary considerably. For example, the mean value is 68.30 percent for rape but fluctuates from 25.74 percent to the extreme of 162.47 percent over the course of the study.

Aggravated assault is similar to rape in that descriptive statistics vary greatly over the study period. The minimum percentage of UCR-recorded crimes compared to reported victimizations in the NCVS is approximately 40 percent, but reaches nearly 160 percent during the period under study. This crime has the highest mean level of reporting amongst the three crime types at nearly 80 percent. Robbery exhibits the least variability. The range is approximately 38 percentage points and the standard deviation is tight by comparison to rape and aggravated assault: 110.7. The mean recording reporting rate is within two percentage points of rape and within twelve of aggravated assault. This appears to be the most stable crime types of the three.

The policing variables are used as indicators of organizational change in the structure and operation of police departments and enforcement activities nationwide. This hypothesis includes variables of two distinct types. The first are variables derived from the UCR and include the utilization of 911,[1] the ratio of aggravated to simple assault, the percentage of the population covered by agencies reporting for 12 months, and the percentage of agencies implementing NIBRS nationwide. Though the mean rate of UCR coverage remains fairly high during the study period, there is variation of nearly 14 percent during the study period.

The percentage of agencies reporting for a full 12 months fluctuates between 87 and 96 percent between 1973 and 1989; however, between 1990 and 2002 the percentage of agencies reporting by a full 12 months is characterized by a general decreasing trend. In 2002 approximately 86 percent of agencies reported for an entire 12 months, down from 89 percent in 1993. These variations are likely due to the implementation of NIBRS, which often produces breaks in full reporting during the transition to the new system.

In contrast to UCR coverage, the coverage indicator for agencies reporting under the NIBRS format shows a steady yearly increase over time. The first year of available NIBRS data is 1991, at which time 1.6 percent of the population was covered by incident-based police reporting. By 2002 this percentage had increased by 15 to 17 percent. Another variable with increasing values over time is the percentage of agencies utilizing 911. By far the greatest variation is seen with this explanatory variable. Though the mean value for 911 participation is 46 percent, this masks the rapidly increasing value associated with the variable. The minimum value is 8.40 percent in 1973 but increases to 89 percent by year 2002. Other UCR related variables show a more gradual increase. For example, the percentage of civilians employed by police agencies increased steadily from 14.6 percent in 1973 to 22 percent in 1990 where it has fluctuated between 1 and 2 percentage points until 2002.

The second set of indicators for police organization is the LEMAS-derived variables that tap into the implementation and extent of computerization in police agencies. As presented in Appendix 1, all LEMAS-derived computerization variables exhibit rapid increases over the last ten years. In 1993 participation in various forms of computerization for investigative and administrative functions ranged from 30 to 45 percent. With the exception of computer usage for police warrants, all variables in this category increased by at least 20 percentage points by 2002.

Descriptive statistics related to the hypothesis of changes in social attitudes are presented in Table 7. Similar to the police organization indicators, these variables may be considered in two categories. First are variables derived from the General Social Survey. Questions asked of respondents were taken from the survey to tap into perceptions and feelings of support for the criminal justice system.

These include perceptions of police ethics, confidence in the police to protect the citizenry, whether penalties of criminal justice courts deal adequately with offenders, and whether respondents can envision any situation in which it is permissible for an officer to strike a citizen.[2]

Of interest in the GSS-derived variables is the public perception of police ethics and confidence in the ability of the police to protect. In both cases the mean level of agreement on these two indicators is

Table 7. Descriptive statistics

Variable	N	Minimum	Maximum	Mean	Std. Deviation
Dependent Variables					
Rape	30	25.74	162.47	68.30	43.19
Robbery	30	46.90	85.30	66.38	11.07
Aggravated assault	30	39.12	159.59	78.64	28.82
Independent Variables					
Year (scaled)	30	1.00	30	15.50	8.80
Police Organization Variables					
UCR coverage	30	82.20	95.60	88.94	3.99
NIBRS	30	.00	17.00	3.27	5.35
Arrest ratio	30	.36	.60	.48	.08
911	30	8.40	89.00	45.69	29.36
Percent civilian	30	14.60	23.40	20.39	2.48
LEMAS in field computers	11	34.00	61.00	50.23	9.47
LEMAS computers record keeping	11	45.00	74.00	60.00	9.56
LEMAS computers criminal investigation	11	30.00	53.00	43.36	7.23
LEMAS computers for arrest	11	39.00	71.00	59.42	11.14
LEMAS computers for warrants	11	31.00	44.0	38.73	4.67
LEMAS personal computers	11	40.00	78.00	58.67	12.10

Social Attitude Variables

Police Ethics	26	37.00	68.00	46.90	6.61
Confidence in Police	22	45.00	70.00	52.63	6.19
Not okay to strike	30	64.00	78.00	30.23	3.91
Courts are harsh enough	30	67.00	85.00	21.02	5.43
Beyond cohabitation	22	5.50	94.6	62.54	28.45
Warrantless arrest	22	1.10	100.00	56.56	32.54
No contact protection order	22	5.80	98.0	69.78	26.97
Victim custody relief	22	5.50	92.3	71.38	27.71
Misdemeanor for PO violation	22	.00	75.90	42.63	24.80
Civil/criminal contempt	22	5.80	74.30	57.58	19.35
Felony for protection order violation	22	.00	4.00	2.43	.91
Mandatory arrest for PO violation	22	.00	61.10	20.77	19.51
Firearm confiscation for PO violation	22	.00	61.00	12.84	21.06

NCVS Design Change Variables

Change in proxy interview	30	0	1	.57	.50
Primary sampling unit reduction	30	0	1	.63	.49
Redesign	30	0	1	.30	.47
Person response rate	30	87.30	98.70	94.69	3.52
Percent CATI	30	.00	30.00	11.33	13.77
Percent telephone	30	20.00	75.00	56.87	22.80
Household response rate	30	92.40	97.00	95.42	1.25

nearly at or above the majority of respondents. In 1973 only 37 percent of respondents agreed that police ethics were either high or very high; however, agreement with this statement increased until 1993 when it reached 50 percent. After experiencing declines over the next two years, the percentage of respondents agreeing that the ethical standards of police were high or very high increased to 68 percent in 2001. This equates to a nearly 30 percentage point change in public perceptions in the ethical character of law enforcement during the period of time examined by this study.

Public confidence in the ability of the police to protect has varied by nearly 35 percentage points during the study period. In 1973 only 49 percent of respondents affirmed their confidence in the ability of the police to offer protection. Following a generally increasing trend, this percentage increased to 70 percent of respondents by 2000. Since then there has been a slight decline, but as of 2002, 58 percent of respondents still state they have confidence in the ability of law enforcement to protect the public from crime. Either of these two variables may be associated with the likelihood that victims may contact the police. If public perception is that the police are ethical, this reflects an assumption that police treatment will be fair.

Additional GSS variables examined include the percentage of respondents stating (1) they could not imagine a situation where a police officer would be justified in striking an adult male, and (2) criminal justice courts dealt adequately with criminals. In 1973 only 27 percent of adult respondents said there were no justifiable situations for police to strike a citizen. This percentage fluctuated between 22 and 27 percent until 1989 whereupon it steadily increased to 36 percent by 2000. Since then there has been a slight decrease back down to 34 percent in 2002. More variability is evident in respondent feelings toward the adequacy of sanctions handed out by criminal justice courts. In 1973, 27 percent of respondents felt that court treatment of offenders was sufficiently punitive. After a brief increase this number declined to 15 percent in 1986, after which time increases upwards of 20 percent were again followed by a decrease in 1994 to 15 percent. Since that time the percentage of respondents agreeing that courts are harsh enough with offenders has increased steadily to a 30 year high of 33 percent in 2002.

The second category of social attitude variables is related to domestic violence legislation. These variables are national level indicators representing the percentage of the U.S. population covered by certain types of domestic violence legislation. All domestic violence variables exhibit rapid increases over time, most notable between the late 1970s and mid-1980s. Beginning in 1976 the percentage of states with any of the identified legislation ranged from 0 to 5.8 percent. By 1997 the various forms of legislation across the states ranged between 42 percent and 100 percent. The one exception is the percentage of states with felony penalties for violations of protection orders, which in 2002 covered only 4 percent of the U.S. population. The rapid increases in these variables are noted in Appendix 1.

The last category of variables presented in Table 7 is related to NCVS design changes. As mentioned previously, including design related changes that affect both series might better suit this hypothesis; however, information regarding UCR design changes is not available for current or past years. Several variables capture administrative and methodological changes to the survey over the study period.

Several of the variables are dichotomous variables. These include the change in proxy interviews, primary sampling unit (PSU) reduction, and the pre- and post-redesign variable. The mean values for these variables range between .30 and .63 and represent the percentage of cases (i.e., years) for which the variable is scored 1. All other variables are measured on an interval scale.

In recent years response rates at the individual and household level have been declining for the NCVS. The person response rate for the NCVS was at its highest level in 1973 when 98.7 percent of all contacted individuals responded to the survey. Since that time there has been a slow and steady decrease in response rates that has reached 87.3 percent in 2002. Household response rates have declined similarly though less drastically. In 1973, 96 percent of sampled households responded to the survey; however, by 2002 this number had declined to 92.4 percent. Though the variation for these variables presented in Table 7 does not seem large, the decline has caused concern for the BJS because the victimization and reporting rates of individuals and households represented by these omitted households is unknown. Thus, though these declines may appear slight in magnitude, the influence on long-term victimization estimates is of import.

Two variables capture changes in the mode of survey administration. CATI was first implemented in 1988. At that time only 5 percent of all interviews were conducted in this manner, but by 2002 that number increased to 30 percent. Similar increases are seen in the number of telephone interviews that are conducted. In 1973 roughly

20 percent of all interviews were conducted over the telephone. This number has increased nearly fourfold to 75 percent in 2002 and will be increasing once more in coming years to alleviate increasing costs associated with in-person interviewing.

STAGE TWO ANALYSIS

Creation of Factor Scores

The number of variables under examination and the presence of multicollinearity amongst the variables make analysis of this sort, or indeed standard statistical models, unwieldy. Factor analysis is one method for distilling the essence of several interrelated variables that may be redundant into fewer statistically uncorrelated variables that retain a linear relationship to the original variables (Gugarati, 1995). For example, in the current study each hypothesis contains several important variables that uniquely contribute to understanding the correspondence in serious violent crime yet may overlap in explanatory power. Factor analysis allows for the extraction of elements from original variables such that the variation explained by extracted factor components is maximized. The hypotheses and supporting indicators presented in this research are well suited for this approach.

Appendix 6 presents the results of factor analyses for variables used in the first stage of analysis. Included in the appendix are basic descriptive statistics, Pearson's correlation matrices, factor loadings, factor scores, and Cronbach's alpha coefficient of reliability for each analysis. The extraction method used is principal component with Varimax rotation using SPSS. In total seven factor analyses were conducted generating six factors. All factor scores were retained for further analysis in the regression format.

The exploratory factor analysis affirmed the categories and groupings of explanatory variables presented thus far. One factor was extracted from the police organization variables. UCR-derived variables loaded highly on the first component while LEMAS computerization variables exhibited high loading on the second component. The first component is operationalized as police technology while the second factor is operationalized as computerization.

Separate analyses were conducted for the social attitude hypothesis. Questions from the GSS loaded highly on one-factor loading and were operationalized as feelings toward the criminal justice system. These included items such as perceptions of police ethics and confidence in the ability of the police to protect. Two factors were extracted from social attitude variables related to domestic violence. Though all the variables deal with changes in the perception of domestic offenses, the loadings of the variables closely mirror the characteristics of victim- and offender-oriented legislation. Some variables are clearly more representative of advocacy intended to aid the victim of abuse (e.g., victim custody relief and protection beyond cohabitation) while others emphasize penalties directed toward the offender (e.g., mandatory arrest and firearm confiscation). These distinctions are logical and are maintained for the remainder of the analysis.

Lastly, factor analysis was conducted on all interval level variables contained within the design change hypothesis. Two factor scores were extracted and retained for further analysis. Dichotomous variables were retained as well. Bivariate correlations between the extracted components and each dependent variable are presented in Appendix 7.

Multivariate Analysis

The second stage of the analysis utilizes multivariate modeling to examine the correspondence between the NCVS and UCR. Three sets of models are estimated in this portion of the analysis. An autoregressive (AR) specification is used in all three instances. For reasons of space and parsimony, only models generating significant effects are reported in text. At this time it was also decided that the LEMAS-related variables be dropped from the analysis because the observable cases do not begin until 1987.

In the first set of models each individual hypothesis is examined separately to conserve degrees of freedom. The results of these models are presented in Table 8. The second set of models presents best fitting models derived from the results of the previous models. These results are presented in Table 9. Following presentation of the best fitting models all significant results are presented in graphical format. This technique offers two analytical benefits. First, graphing allows for a visual appraisal of the relationship between significant explanatory and dependent variables. Second, this approach allows for presentation of the decomposed variables against the explanatory variables. Lastly, the significant results of the best fitting models are further examined in Table 10, which models the dependent variable in a decomposed format similar to that presented in Graphs 3-10. The statistical package SPSS was used. Before presenting the findings for the multivariate analysis, the characteristics of the data and the implications for modeling are discussed.

Modeling and Data Issues

The requirements for ordinary least squares (OLS) models are that no perfect multicollinearity exists, the error term is independent and identically distributed, and that the model is theoretically informed (Gugarati, 1995; Johnston and DiNardo, 1997). There are two tests designed to diagnose these problems. The variance inflation factor (VIF) assesses the extent of multicollinearity amongst the variables. The Durbin-Watson test is used to identify whether serial correlation is present in the model. Rather than using a time series model this analysis begins by examining the results and diagnostics of OLS models.

An assumption of OLS is that the dependent and independent variables are fixed in their parameters. For time series data this concept is equal to that of stationarity. If the underlying data process is now fixed in time, or stationary, it may be estimated with fixed coefficients (Hamilton, 1994; Pindyck and Rubinfeld, 1998). Preliminary models were first estimated using the OLS version of a linear estimator.

Preliminary models are first estimated using the OLS version of a linear estimator. In general, using factor analysis assists considerably with degrees of freedom. However, the Durbin-Watson statistics indicate that the models are autocorrelated. The time series data were characterized with few degrees of freedon so little modeling maneuverability was available. Rather than lose additional observations through differencing, the lagged dependent variable is introduced on the right side of the equation. Subsequent examination of the residuals indicated that the autocorrelation function (ACF) and partial autocorrelation function (PACF) were within tolerable parameters.

Further diagnostics in the preliminary models indicate high levels of multicollinearity. Multicollinearity will produce erroneous conclusions regarding the significance of explanatory variables. Examination of an F-change statistic is a method used by researchers to ascertain the relative influence of explanatory variables as they are entered into the model. An F-change statistic allows investigators to evaluate the change in the R^2, F statistic, and whether change in the F score significantly improves the explanatory power of the model (Granato,

1996; Pindyck and Rubinfeld, 1998). The F-change statistic is included for each of the models evaluated in the current research.

Because the data measure change over time they are formally defined as time series data. Ostom (9:1978) defines time series as "a collection of data of the form X (t=1,2...,T) with the interval between X_t and $X_t=1$ [as] fixed and constant." The low degree of freedom means there is little room to work with; however, there are several ways to address time dependency when modeling AR models. Two such ways include taking the first difference of the dependent variable and incorporating a lag of the dependent variable on the right hand side of the equation. The benefit of lagging the dependent variable is that it conserves degrees of freedom and eases interpretation of the coefficients. After examining several different specifications, I decided to use the general form:

$$Y = \alpha + \beta (y_{t-1}) + \beta x_1 ... + \beta x_k + e$$

Following this specification additional models were estimated and the residuals of these models examined to check for stationarity. ACF and PACF graphs of the residuals indicated that the series were stationary. With stationarity induced through a lag procedure the need to difference variables was precluded from the analysis and the degrees of freedom were conserved. The results of the ACF and PACF suggest that the data are characterized by a time dependency but this is adequately controlled for by an AR(1) specification.

AR(1) Models

Table 8 presents the findings for the first set of models. The first set of models examined each dependent variable and individual hypothesis. Only two models produced findings that attained conventional levels of significance. First, variables related to the hypotheses of social attitudes and NCVS design change were significantly related to the convergence in rape. Second, variables related to social attitudes and NCVS design change were significantly related to the convergence in aggravated assault.

Findings for the influence of social attitudes for rape are examined first. This hypothesis states that feelings toward the criminal justice system and increased domestic violence legislation are positively related to the correspondence between police recording and victim reporting of rape. Model 1 presents these findings. In this model only one

Table 8. The effect of social attitudes and NCVS design change on UCR and NCVS convergence, 1973-2002

RAPE		Unstandardized	Standard Error	Standardized	VIF
Model 1: Social Attitudes					
	Feelings toward CJ	-23.81*	11.54	-.269	2.16
	Victim oriented legislation	22.56	15.36	.18	1.84
	Offender oriented legislation	33.33*	9.32	1.04	10.78
	Lagged rape variable	.17	.32	.164	12.43
	Constant	31.76	26.60		
	adj. R^2	.87			
Model 2: NCVS Design Change					
	NCVS response	-16.94*	7.69	-.39	10.15
	NCVS technology	27.15**	8.54	.62	12.00
	Change in proxy interview	5.75	12.88	.07	7.07
	PSU reduction	-9.52	10.67	-.11	4.52
	Redesign	56.04**	17.52	.61	11.55
	Lagged rape variable	-.58**	.21		13.62
	Constant	92.24***	14.53		
	adj. R^2	.91			

AGGRAVATED ASSAULT		Unstandardized	Standard Error	Standardized	VIF
Model 1: Social Attitudes	Feelings toward cj system	-2.120	6.52	-.05	2.33
	Victim oriented legislation	18.77*	6.29	.50	1.91
	Offender oriented legislation	8.75*	3.40	.63	5.91
	Lagged aggravated assault variable	.27	.28	.27	5.15
	Constant	48.24*	21.23		
	adj. R^2	.80			
Model 2: NCVS Design Change	NCVS response	-11.92*	5.45	-.42	10.53
	NCVS technology	-2.02	6.34	-.07	13.86
	Change in proxy interview	7.68	8.99	.14	7.11
	PSU reduction	-1.08	7.44	-.02	4.54
	Redesign	-8.98	10.85	-.15	10.53
	Lagged assault variable	.77	.19	.68	8.18
	Constant	20.32	15.83		
	adj. R^2	.90			

$*p<.05$
$**p<.01$
$***p<.001$

79

coefficient generated a significant effect. The summary measure for offender oriented legislation is positively related to the convergence for rape (β=33.3; p < .05). Thus as the percentage of the U.S. population covered by this type of legislation has increased, so too has greater correspondence between police recording and victim reporting of rape. The VIF scores in model 1 are within tolerable parameters. The adjusted R- square is .87, indicating that approximately 87 percent of the variation in the dependent variable is explained by the dependent variables.

The second model examined for rape addresses the hypothesis of NCVS design change. Three coefficients generated significant effects in this model. First, the summary measure for NCVS level of response is negatively related to the correspondence (β=16.94; p < .05). This is not surprising considering that fewer respondents to the survey questionnaire decrease the number of rapes captured by the survey. Second, the increased use of technology in the NCVS (i.e. CATI and telephone interviewing) is positively related to greater correspondence (β=27.15; p < .05). Lastly, the redesign of the NCVS is significantly related to increased correspondence (β=56.04; p < .01).

The redesign and increased use of NCVS technology were implemented to capture difficult to detect crimes and circumvent interviewer error that affects the accuracy of data collection. These results indicate that implementation of these changes produced the desired effect of greater precision in data collection. The lag of the dependent variable is significant indicating that time dependency is an issue in this model. Neither change in the proxy interview status of PSU reduction attains conventional levels of significance. The VIF scores for this model are slightly higher than in the previous model yet remain within tolerable parameters. The adjusted R-square is .91 indicating that 91 percent of the variation in the dependent variable is explained by the independent variables.

The second crime examined in Table 8 is the crime of aggravated assault. Variables related to the same two hypotheses for rape are significantly related to the correspondence in aggravated assault. Model 1 presents the results for variables related to social attitudes. In this model the coefficient for victim-oriented (β=18.77; p < .05) and offender-oriented (β=8.75; p < .05) generate significant effects. The results indicate that increases in domestic violence legislation are positively associated with the correspondence in police-recorded and victim-reported aggravated assault. The second model examines aggravated assault. The only coefficient to attain conventional levels of significance is NCVS response. Not surprisingly, the relationship is negative indicating that decreased response rates are associated with decreased correspondence between the UCR and NCVS for the crime of aggravated assault. The lack of significant findings in the AR models, especially for robbery, may be due to the small number of cases available for analysis. As additional years of data become available for analysis this suspicion may be tested further, since a time series of thirty years is vulnerable to significant changes in inference resulting from small changes in specification.

Best Fitting Models

Table 9 presents two full models for rape and aggravated assault. For the model examining rape, coefficients for the design-related variables all generated a significant effect, but the effect of offender-based legislation on the dependent variable was washed out with the inclusion of these additional variables. The direction of each design-related coefficient remained the same though the degree of significance increased for both NCVS response and technology.

The lagged rape variable remained significant. VIF scores were within tolerable parameters. For models in Table 9, R-square change statistics are presented directly below the respective model. For the first model the change summary indicates that with the exception of the offender-based legislation, the addition of each subsequent variable added to the explanatory power of the model.

In the best fitting model for aggravated assault the only coefficient to attain significance is for the variable of victim-oriented legislation. The effects of both offender-based legislation and NCVS response are washed out when controlled for simultaneously. Additionally, the magnitude of the variable is attenuated somewhat, though the level of significance remains the same. Regardless, two central findings were robust across all specifications: the effect of design change on rape and the effect of domestic violence legislation on aggravated assault.

Table 9. Best fitting models for NCVS and UCR convergence

RAPE	Unstandardized	Standard Error	Standardized	VIF
Lagged rape variable	-.20	.21	-.19	20.13
Feelings toward CJ	-5.89	6.84	-.07	2.92
Offender oriented legislation	-.30	7.98	-.01	30.47
NCVS response	-28.69***	5.78	-.57	7.18
NCVS technology	23.87**	6.12	.48	7.40
NCVS redesign	19.47	16.11	.24	18.89
Constant	72.41***	13.37		
adj. R²	.97			

Change Statistics

Model	R square change	F change	df1	df2	Sig. F change
1	.776	51.864	1	15	.000
2	.014	.938	1	14	.352
3	.099	11.578	1	13	.005
4	.059	13.384	1	12	.003
5	.029	13.757	1	11	.003
6	.003	1.462	1	10	.254

AGGRAVATED ASSAULT	Unstandardized	Standard Error	Standardized	VIF
Lagged assault variable	.30	.26	.31	10.02
Victim oriented legislation	8.71*	3.75	.47	5.86
Offender oriented legislation	11.96	6.68	.65	18.54
NCVS response	5.83	6.67	.21	8.08
Constant	50.08**	17.70		
adj. R^2	.85			

Change Statistics

Model	R square change	F change	df1	df2	Sig. F change
1	.835	101.528	1	20	.000
2	.009	1.061	1	19	.326
3	.030	4.288	1	18	.053
4	.005	.763	1	17	.395

*p<.05
**p<.01
***p<.001

Graphs

In this stage of the analysis independent variables from the best fitting models are graphed against the dependent variables. For example, the first dependent variable to be examined is for the crime of rape. For this crime each variable is graphed against the crime of rape. The dependent variable is generated as a percentage of a UCR-derived denominator and a NCVS-derived numerator. While this construction is informative in assessing relative NCVS and UCR values, the relationship of these series to each individual hypothesis may be suppressed or dominated by substantial increases or decreases in either the numerator or denominator. In this manner factors and hypotheses exerting greater influence on one series or the other will be visually apparent.

Figures 3-6 present graphs for the dependent variable of rape. Figure 3 presents the dependent variables for rape graphed against the factor scores for the feelings toward the criminal justice system and offender-based legislation. Clearly in this figure there is agreement in the behavior of the dependent variable and factor scores over time with both factor scores influencing the behavior of the dependent variable over time. Figure 4 presents the dependent variable decomposed into its component elements. In this format both summary measures appear more strongly related to the NCVS and UCR.

Figure 3 shows a stronger similarity between UCR rape counts and offender oriented legislation. However, the two seemingly diverge in the early 1990s. Feelings toward the criminal justice system appears to follow a dissimilar path than the UCR until the early 1980s, at which time this summary measure increases more rapidly than the UCR. Taken together though, the two continue to trend upward until the early 1990s. At that time the summary measures for criminal justice support increase exponentially.

Figure 5 and 6 present the factor scores for NCVS technology and response graphed against the dependent variable and component parts for rape. Once again the dependent variable masks the true relationship over time. In Figure 5 there appears to be little relationship over time. Yet in turning to Figure 6 we see that the factor scores for both design change measures directly follow the behavior of the NCVS rather than the UCR. The correspondence for rape is motivated primarily by a rapid decrease in rape counts reported to interviewers during the survey process. Very little of the correspondence is attributable to changing increases in the UCR recording of rape. Thus even though the police currently record more rapes than are reported to them (or reported in the NCVS, for that matter), this appears to be an artifact of changes in the NCVS rather than variables that affect UCR counts of rape.

Figure 7 presents the dependent variable for aggravated assault and the summary measures for domestic violence legislation. The most notable correspondence examined so far is evident between offender-based legislation and the dependent variable for aggravated assault. Relying solely on the information in this figure is misleading, however, as the picture changes somewhat in Figure 8. As was apparent with rape, the convergence for aggravated assault appears to be motivated primarily by steady increases in the recording of aggravated assault by enforcement personnel coupled with a steady and then more rapidly declining number of aggravated assaults reported to NCVS interviewers.

When graphed against the decomposed variable the influence of both victim- and offender-oriented legislation is evident. For victim-related legislation the value for the score is low in the early 1970s but increases rapidly, surpassing the UCR count after which point the behavior of the UCR trend follows the steadily upward movement of the offender legislation factor. The summary measure for offender-oriented legislation stabilizes during the time period that both the victim oriented and UCR are increasing, though toward the late 1980s this factor score as well begins to increase in conjunction with the UCR count.

Lastly the same pattern is observed for aggravated assault and the NCVS response measure. In Figure 9 there appears to be no similarity between the two trends. They appear to be converging prior to 1993 at which time after crossing over they begin to diverge. When examined in decomposed form (Figure 10) we see that the response measure declines more rapidly than both UCR and NCVS counts of aggravated assault. In recent years the UCR has recorded more aggravated assaults than captured by the NCVS. Though the decline in NCVS aggravated assault is not as extreme as the decline seen in the crime of rape, it is evident that the convergence in aggravated assault is motivated by a more rapidly declining NCVS count than changes in the UCR (Hart and Rennison, 2003).

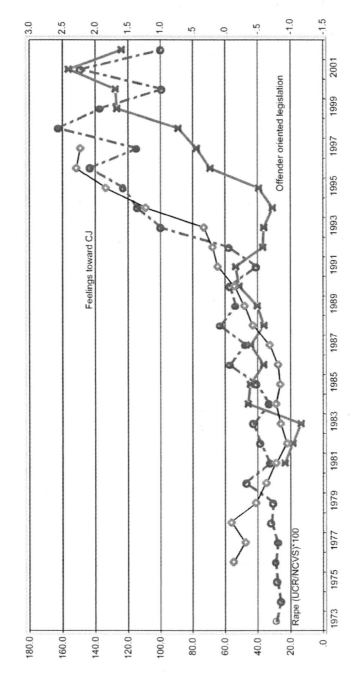

Figure 3. Rape (UCR/NCVS)*100 and social attitudes

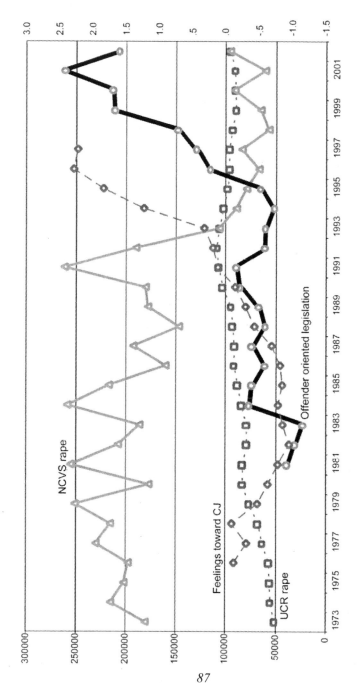

Figure 4. NCVS and UCR rape and social attitudes

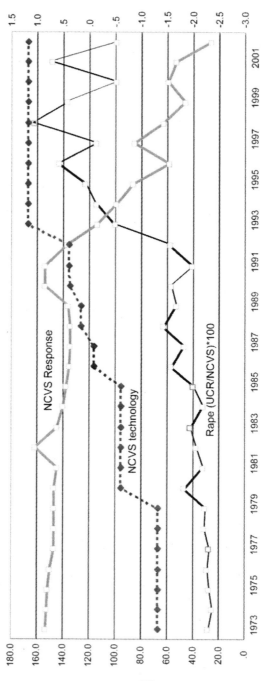

Figure 5. Rape (UCR/NCVS)*100 and NCVS response

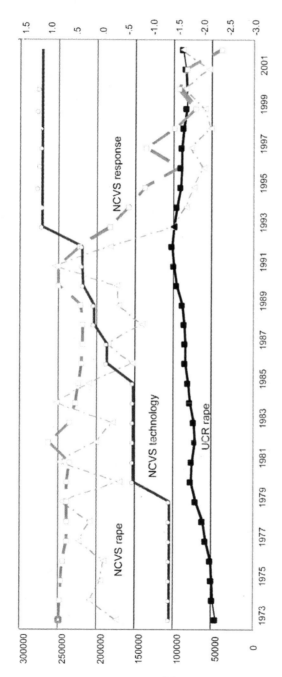

Figure 6. NCVS and UCR rape and NCVS response

89

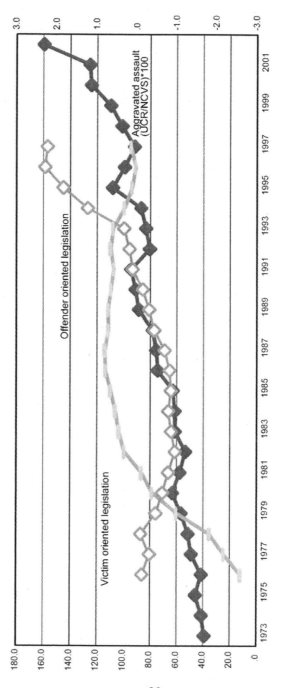

Figure 7. Aggravated assault and (UCR/NCVS)*100 and social attitudes

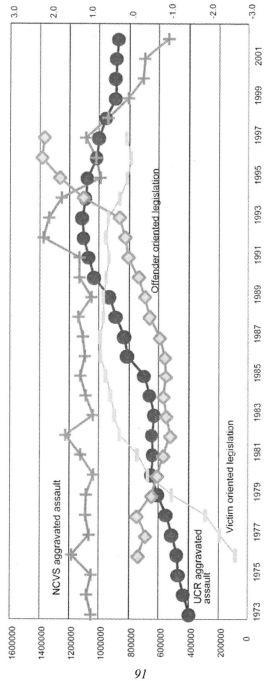

Figure 8. NCVS and UCR aggravated assault and social attitudes

91

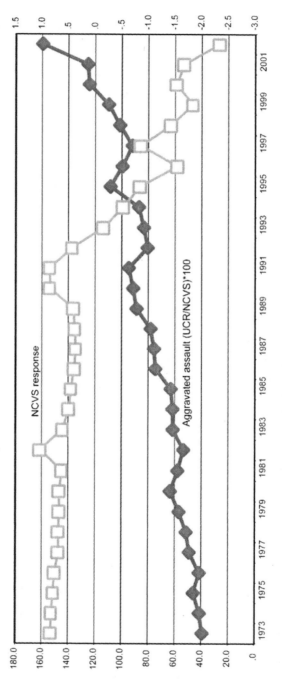

Figure 9. Aggravated assault (UCR/NCVS)*100 and NCVS response

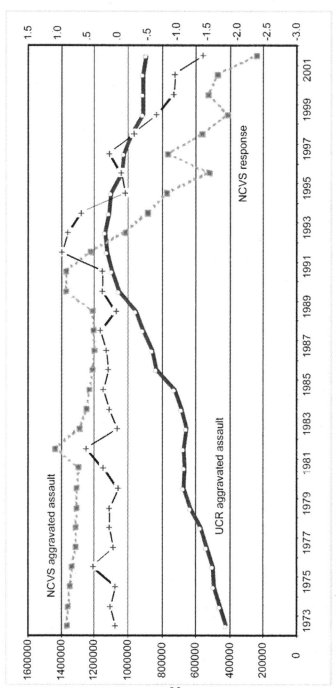

Figure 10. NCVS and UCR aggravated assault and NCVS response

Decomposed Models

The last step of the analysis is to model the graphed relationships using the decomposed variables. Table 10 presents these results. These results indicate that design related variables affect the NCVS series while summary measures intended to capture social change are more likely to influence the UCR series. No support was found in previous models to support the first hypothesis of changes in policing. The results of the decomposed models indicate that with respect to increased correspondence for rape and aggravated assault, changes in policing are contributing in some manner to improved reporting over time. Additionally in Model 1, the influence of feelings toward the criminal justice system is now positive whereas in the model presented in Table 8, the influence on the dependent variables was negative.

Table 10. Decomposed UCR and NCVS models

RAPE	Unstandardized	Standard Error	Standardized	VIF
Model 1: UCR Rape Count				
Feelings toward CJ	7417.92**	1909.97	.32	1.748
Offender oriented legislation	-1571.48	1853.44	-.19	12.580
NCVS response	2953.03	2192.39	.22	7.119
NCVS technology	763.99	3742.65	.06	21.198
Lagged rape variable	.968***	.170	1.00	8.119
Constant	6706.84	14819.58		
adj. R^2	.94			
Model 2: NCVS Rape Count				
Feelings toward CJ	32345.70	23704.71	.20	1.734
Offender oriented legislation	17309.50	23695.62	.30	13.239
NCVS response	71023.06*	24829.03	.79	5.879
NCVS technology	-56580.36*	23212.46	-.64	5.250
Lagged rape variable	-.01	.22	-.06	3.269
Constant	193812.62***	64.46		
adj. R^2	.79			

AGGRAVATED ASSAULT	Unstandardized	Standard Error	Standardized	VIF
Model 1: UCR Aggravated Assault Count				
Victim oriented legislation	157201.14***	21457.28	.721	1.306
Offender oriented legislation	242798.24***	44727.76	1.11	5.675
NCVS response	149542.27*	74402.37	.45	6.859
Lagged agg. assault variable	.93	.62	.17	1.762
Constant	776859.35***	27952.05		
adj. R^2	.84			
Model 2: NCVS Aggravated Assault Count				
Victim oriented legislation	21449.42	21229.84	.219	1.226
Offender oriented legislation	27369.90	46677.31	.280	5.926
NCVS response	45370.63	73621.87	.31	6.439
Lagged agg. assault variable	.46*	.19	.52	1.122
Constant	48.235*	21.231		
adj. R^2	.19			

*p<.05
**p<.01
***p<.001

97

CHAPTER 6

The NCVS and UCR Convergence

Crime occupies a central position in contemporary American discourse. Indeed, it is one of the few topics on which everyone agrees: Less crime is better. Where discussions about crime become contentious is the manner in which as a society we attempt to increase our understanding and actively use this knowledge to reduce crime. There are currently two national-level indicators that inform the public and policy makers about levels of crime in American society.

The UCR, sponsored by law enforcement, provides our earliest estimates of crime. A frequent criticism of the program, however, is that it ultimately reflects how police respond to crime rather than providing an objective assessment on the nature of crime. The UCR was first intended as a way for police agencies to monitor levels of crime but later assumed greater importance as the public began to view crime as an indicator of social well-being. In contrast, the second indicator of crime, the NCVS, measures crime in a distinctly different manner. Unlike the UCR, the NCVS generates survey-based estimates rather than an estimate based on administrative records. The benefit of the victimization survey is that information is asked of victims and non-victims and those who report the crime to the police and those who do not. Taken together these two programs have occupied a central, though sometimes contentious, position in how crime is portrayed and understood in the United States.

Because the NCVS and UCR estimate the extent and nature of crime in different ways, there has been a reluctant acceptance that the data derived from each source will differ. For many years researchers tried to explain why the two series should and would present different pictures of the national crime trends (Biderman and Lynch, 1991; Cohen and Land, 1984; Gove, Hughes, and Geerken, 1985; McDowall and Loftin, 1992). An important question for current research is to ask how, and more importantly why, after twenty years of relative divergence, the two series have now converged, at least in absolute numbers. This study filled a previous gap in the literature by examining this question. Four hypotheses were posited to explain the increased correspondence between the two data measures: (1) changes in policing, (2) changes in the demographic composition of the population, (3) changes in the social perception of crime, and (4) changes in the methodological design of the NCVS.

Following preliminary examination of the second hypothesis, I ascertained that there was not sufficient variability in demographic characteristics to explain the increased correspondence between the two series, at least at the national level. This hypothesis was dropped from further consideration. Second, changes in the administration of the UCR were not measurable, and thus I focused on changes in the NCVS that were quantifiable and transparent by comparison to the UCR.

The analysis was comprised of several parts. Following examination of individual graphs of each variable, exploratory factor analyses were used to examine the characteristics of the data and reduce the number of independent variables. Relationships between the hypothesized influential factors and the dependent variables were then modeled using multivariate analysis. From these preliminary models best fitting models were then generated. Additional insight was gained by decomposing the dependent variable into the constituent parts and again examining the graphs to ascertain whether additional relationships between individual factor scores and the dependent variable were masked by the construction of the dependent variables as a ratio of one series to another.

Lastly, multivariate models were estimated for previously identified significant findings but were now estimated with decomposed versions of the dependent variable. In all cases the relationships were modeled using an AR(1) specification that, according to ACF and PACFs, adequately controlled for time dependency amongst the variables. All findings reported in the previous chapter were robust across all stages of the analysis. Influential variables identified early in the analysis were robust across all stages of the analysis.

One limitation of the research is that the short number of years for analysis place restrictions on the complexity of time series methods that may be used. Hence it is possible that the AR-based models used in this study washed out effects of influential variables. Yet two central findings remained consistent throughout all stages of the analysis. First, design-related changes in the NCVS were negatively associated with the correspondence in rape. Second, victim-oriented and offender-oriented legislation were positively related to the convergence between victim-reported and police-recorded aggravated assault. These two findings and their implications for further research are summarized in the following sections.

SUMMARY OF FINDINGS

After decomposing serious violent crime into the component offenses of rape, robbery, and aggravated assault, the resulting graphs of rape, robbery, and aggravated assault indicated that using an aggregate measure of serious violent crime obscured crime-specific variation. Indeed, in viewing serious violent crimes as a combined measure of the three, the crime of aggravated assault dominated both the visual graphs as well as bivariate and multivariate analysis.[1] This finding was not surprising. Although any violent crime is a relatively rare occurrence, aggravated assault is by far the most frequently occurring of the three offenses, and the findings of any analysis will be driven primarily by the magnitude of aggravated assault. Blumstein (1998, 2000) argues that disaggregation is requisite in any research of index crime because minor fluctuations in a crime such as aggravated assault will overwhelm the variability of other crimes. This finding was observed in the present study as well.

Two central and robust findings emerged from the research for two crimes: rape and aggravated assault. I begin by discussing the findings for aggravated assault because ostensibly this crime has driven the national convergence between the NCVS and UCR. Recall that the BJS provides only a summary measure of the increased correspondence in serious violent crime, and that to date no research has identified the underlying factors responsible for the unprecedented NCVS and UCR convergence. The primary finding of this research is that convergence between reported victimizations and police-recorded crimes is motivated by changes in police recording of aggravated assault. Additionally, the increased correspondence is significantly related to increases in the presence of legislation directed toward domestic violence.

Between 1973 and 1990, the increasing correspondence between reporting and recording appears primarily driven by relative increases in the level of police recording (BJS, 2002). Though levels of victim reporting have increased five percent from their 1973 levels, overall levels of recording by the police have increased 116 percent from 1973 to 1995 (Rand, Lynch, and Cantor, 1997). This result strongly suggests that organizational change in the manner that police respond to and record crime (Black, 1970; Kitsuse and Cicourel, 1963; Langan and Farrington, 1998; McCleary, Bienstadt, and Erven, 1982), specifically for aggravated assault, contributes to increased correspondence between the NCVS and UCR.

Though one may first expect these changes to be evident n the variables intended to capture policing changes (i.e., derived from the UCR), recall that the variables for police organization, percentage of 911 usage and percentage of civilian workforce variables, focused strictly on UCR derived indicators of administrative change. Perhaps the best variable intended to capture changes in aggravated assault—the ratio of aggravated to simple assault arrests—generated no significant effect when examined in the multivariate context.

Significant effects were not found in policing organization variables but instead for indicators intended to capture changes in social perceptions. This implies that rather than upgrading previously captured assaults, the police may now be recording incidents that were not previously recorded at all. Unfortunately, this question is beyond the scope of the present research and the data do not permit further examination of this hypothesis. However, the question of upgrading versus newly recorded crime provides an opportunity for researchers to examine how changes in police response to crime are related to broader social change over time.

In examining trends in aggravated assault over time, three variables were positively associated with the increased correspondence: victim- and offender-oriented legislation directed toward the crime of domestic violence, and the summary measure for NCVS response rates. The NCVS response is, not surprisingly, negatively related to increased correspondence between the NCVS and UCR. The extent of this relationship is that decreased survey response widens the gap between police-recorded and victim-reported crime. In contrast, the more intriguing contributor to congruity for aggravated assault is the effect of changes in the percentage of the U.S. population covered by certain forms of intimate partner violence legislation. Though these legislative initiatives are symbolic of changing social perceptions about domestic violence, it is reasonable to assume that they also influence police responses to this offense, at least over the long term. After all, for legislation to have the desired effect, recourse to enforcement under penalty of law must be present.

In the end, those who enforce the law, namely the police and courts, are ultimately responsible for making changes to accommodate new legislation stemming from broader-based social perceptions in the definition and response to crime. This is true whether the response is warrantless arrest, increased use of protection orders, mandatory arrest, or firearm confiscation for protection order violations. Additionally changes in intimate partner violence may play proxy for other police responses to certain crime types. For instance, informative research is forthcoming to better understand the influence of weapons use in aggravated assault and how it in turn influences police response and subsequent recording of crime (Rosenfeld, 2006).

Hence changes in response to domestic violence may not be solely responsible for changes in police recording practice. As Rosenfeld (2006) suggests, differences over time in the categorization of aggravated assault may represent an upgrading of crimes that were previously handled informally or categorized as simple assault. This need not be limited to legislation directed toward violence between intimates. Indeed, a factor not considered by the present research may exert a greater effect on police recording overall, not simply aggravated assault.

This notion is touched upon in previous research as well. Dugan (2003) examined the connections between domestic violence legislation and subsequent involvement of and arrest by police. Surprisingly, she found that fewer laws actually increased police involvement, no laws were associated with more domestic violence arrests, and mandatory laws may reduce the number of cases entering the system. While these associations may seem contradictory, the findings suggest that situations with diverse characteristics contribute differentially to the ratio of aggravated to simple assault arrest. Further, Dugan (2002:299) finds that "police were informed of less than half of all domestic violence incidents suggesting that the 'dark figure' in domestic violence is about the same as what is known to police." Such findings reinforce the argument that intimate partner violence cases along are not responsible for the upturn in aggravated assault arrests (see also Dugan, Nagin, and Rosenfeld, 2003).

The second consistent finding uncovered in this research is that increased correspondence for rape is negatively associated with changes in the NCVS design. In the preliminary models two relationships were present that later either washed out or were further qualified. In Table 8, support for the criminal justice system was negatively related to the correspondence in rape, and offender-oriented legislation was positively associated to the increased correspondence. Significant effects for both of these variables washed out when controlling simultaneously for NCVS related design changes. However, in the decomposed models (Table 10), support for the criminal justice system was significantly and *positively* related to police recording:rape of rape over time. Though not influential in the increased correspondence, this variable is positively associated with the increased recording of this crime to the police over time. This indicates a greater willingness of persons to contact the police as general support for the criminal justice system increases.

A more robust finding for rape is the relationship between NCVS-related design change and the correspondence in rape. The crime of rape is problematic for analysis especially when using the NCVS: as presented in the graphs of Appendix 1, point estimates of rape in the NCVS are strongly influenced by sample size. Consequently, the results of the present study should be taken with a grain of salt. One purpose of the NCVS redesign was to increase reporting of victimizations by intimates and acquaintances, and two crimes in which victimization by acquaintances or intimates are likely to occur are assault and rape. In the case of rape results changed between original AR(1) models and the final decomposed models.

Recall that the two summary measures for NCVS redesign were comprised of person and household response rates which have been declining within the last decade, and technological measures that have been increasing within the last decade—the percentage of CATI and telephone interviews. There is an intuitive and conceptual appeal to the notion that these countervailing changes will be negatively and positively related to the correspondence, respectively. The true effect of declining response rates on crime estimates remains unknown since the characteristics of individuals omitted from the survey and reasons for non-contact are beyond the ability of the present data to discern. Of all current surveys sponsored by the Federal government, the NCVS rates of no one home or other form of non-contact comprise the largest portion of initial non-response (Atrostic, Bates, Burt, and Silberstein; 2001; Groves and Couper, 1998).

With respect to NCVS technology, a positive relationship is observed in the model testing the hypothesis of design change and in the best fitting model presented in Table 9. Thus, as the percentage of CATI and telephone interviews increases, a significant increase in the correspondence between the two series is in evidence. Research has shown that CATI and telephone interviewing generate higher victimization counts primarily due to the fact that interviewers are not able to accidentally skip out of sections, thereby omitting relevant victimizations.

Less intuitive is the changing relationship between these summary measures in the decomposed models for rape. Both summary measures retain conventional levels of significance but the nature of the relationship changes. NCVS response is positively associated with NCVS rape counts while NCVS technology is negatively associated with NCVS rape counts. With respect to NCVS response, the relationship is intuitive. As NCVS technology increases the correspondence between the UCR and NCVS increases. The negative relationship between NCVS technology and increased correspondence in rape is less apparent. Considering the influence of increased CATI and telephone interviewing, the expected relationship is positive.

However, this result may be confounded by two factors. First, the relative rarity of rape as a crime in the NCVS (and the volatility of yearly estimates) combined with the fact that technology has been steadily increasing over time while the NCVS count for rape has been steadily decreasing. Returning to Graph 6 of the previous chapter, the extent of this relationship is evident. Thus, rather than technology *causing* fewer incidents to be captured in the NCVS, there are simply fewer instances of rape to be captured despite technological innovations to gain more precise estimates in the NCVS.[2]

LIMITATIONS AND FUTURE RESEARCH

The significance of the findings reported above must be considered in conjunction with the limited number of time points available for time-series analysis. Though the UCR has reported data about crime since the 1930s, the NCVS is only now entering its thirtieth year. The types of time series analyses that can be made are therefore limited generally to AR(1) models that are able to control for time dependency. This limitation will diminish in importance as time passes and more years are available for analysis.

Second, this study examined the increased congruence between the police recording and victim reporting of serious violent crime at the national level. What remains unknown is whether relationships present at the national level mask variation at the regional or state level. Forthcoming research (Lauritsen and Langan, 2004) suggests that the effect of changes across counties and metropolitan standard area (MSA) units may differ from what is observed at the national level. Consequently, future investigators should carefully examine other levels of analyses as well to evaluate whether similar patterns exist.

Subsequent studies would therefore require area-identified NCVS data and UCR data at the MSA and county level. Though UCR county level data is available, NCVS data at less than the regional level was not available to me at the beginning of my research. Despite a wealth of potential information such analyses might reveal, questions regarding the reliability of county-level UCR data from different locales would need to be addressed (Maltz, 1999; Maltz and Targonski 2002). Especially important would be analyses of UCR and NCVS trends in aggravated assaults at the state level where investigators could control for differences in domestic violence legislation across states.

This study was only able to examine aggravated assault as a category without distinguishing differences across various incidents.

Future research would be served by a disaggregation of this crime into victim-offender categories. Currently only two types of assault arrest categories are reported in *Crime in the United States*: aggravated assault and other assault, a category that includes all simple assaults (Cynthia Barnett, FBI, personal communication). It is plausible that police are increasingly focused on one type of assaultive behavior, such as family violence. For example, multiple variations of crime incidents may now be classified by police agencies. Thus, upgrading alone does not account for the increase in these arrests but inclusion of incidents previously omitted from official statistics altogether.

For instance, domestic violence cases previously handled informally or categorized as simple assault might now be upgraded to aggravated assault. Second, other forms of assaultive behavior (e.g., bar fights, threats with firearms, arguments among neighbors) previously not captured by official statistics are more likely to be recorded by police officers (Rosenfeld, 2002). Domestic violence alone may not account for increases in police recording but may tap into broader changes in how police go about responding to crime. These nuances in the crime of aggravated assault could be disentangled by use of a victim-offender distinction within the crime type.

Moreover, the indicators of police behavior used in this study proved to be rough proxies of administrative and organizational change. Though no better data currently exist at the national level, future research might focus upon operational behaviors that directly dictate the behavior of the police, such as legislative mandates. The results of this research suggest that behavioral and administrative changes in policing may tap into much deeper organizational characteristics of law enforcement than this study was able to address.

One final statement must be made about the national-level focus of this research. In some cases data from the state level were aggregated to the national level, such as with the domestic violence legislation, but in many instances data available for smaller units of analysis cannot be aggregated to the national level. For instance, the mobility of high-risk population in the NCVS may be counted by calculating the percentage of mover relocating out of sample after one or two interviews. Yet it is unclear what this calculation would contribute to this study at the national level. Aside from the complexity of extracting such a number across thirty years of NCVS data files, reconciling these figures with the panel nature of surveys would be a monumental task (but see Dugan, 1999). Several proxy measures (none of which were easy to attain) were used to address these concerns, such as the percentage of the population in jail and prison and the percentage of unbounded interviews from the NCVS. Hence, this study was constantly balancing between what was relevant and achievable while being theoretically informative.

CONCLUSION

One question currently asked is whether the nation requires two measures of crime if the UCR and NCVS are now in agreement regarding the level of crime in the country. If after thirty years the police now record all crimes reported by victims, are both programs needed? This study examined the broad empirical and methodological issues involved in the measurement of serious violent crime. But as a social phenomenon crime can never be directly measured. As such we rely on the measures we have created to attempt to understand the nature and extent of the true crime rate. This is reflected in the dependent variable used by this research: crimes that police recorded by police and crimes that victims reported to police. Recall that the total number of violent crimes recorded by the NCVS (reported and not reported to the police) is still greater than that recorded by the UCR. Though trends for total crime captured by the NCVS and crimes recorded by police are converging in recent years, we must still be suspicious that perfect correspondence is inevitable.

Additionally, the decreasing distance between the two series is directly related to the crime drop between 1992 and 2002. During this time the overall number of crimes reported to police declined marginally, while the number of crimes that were not reported to the police decreased substantially (Hart and Rennison, 2003). Once crime begins to rise again there is no guarantee that the series will not again diverge.

Furthermore, there still exist issues with missing data and the UCR. Research (Maltz and Targonski, 2002; Maltz, 1999) shows that missing data influence crime estimates at the national and county level. Thus working with county-level data without a full understanding of the data limitations is problematic. Several issues related to UCR data and population characteristics might affect estimates derived from analyses with this data.

For instance, crime levels at the county level are allocated from a central statewide location to each individual county. These allotments are based on the proportion of the county population as compared to the entire state and are not based directly on reporting from each individual county. With respect to population data characteristics, imputation strategies used by the FBI remain poorly documented. There are instances of double counting, such as when smaller agencies are covered by larger agencies (Maltz and Targonski, 2000). The effect of this "missingness" at the national level remains unknown (Maltz 1999); however, it emphasizes the incomplete nature of UCR estimates.

Moreover, in recent years decreases in sample size and response rates in the NCVS have increased the reliance on an alternate measure to fill in the gap. These two factors influence the precision of the estimates derived from the survey more in the past decade. Decreasing sample size will generate wider confidence intervals around victimization estimates therefore increasing congruence. In contrast, decreasing response rates might affect sample representativeness. It is important to remember that estimates derived from the NCVS are based on a survey design, and to an unknown extent, the appearance of increased congruence may be an artifact of sampling error. To assume the UCR and NCVS tell the same story and rely on one measure is a mistake.

The primary impetus for the NCVS may be found in the following quote from the 1967 Presidential Commission on Law Enforcement and the Administration of Justice:

> If we knew more about the characteristics of both offenders and victims, the nature of their relationships and the circumstances that create a high probability of criminal conduct, it seems likely that crime prevention and control programs could be made much more effective.

The purpose of the survey was to create a picture of the *nature and extent* of criminal victimization. If as a society we were merely interested in long-term trends in crime, then perhaps the UCR would suffice. The UCR is simply incapable of providing the depth of detail regarding nonfatal violence that is provided by the NCVS. For example, the UCR is unable to provide information on victim perceptions of the offender, whether and to whom victimizations are reported, simple assaults, domestic violence, and crime that remains *unreported* to law enforcement.

Most importantly two measures are required because crime is important in American society. Reliance on one method of observing crime might be similarly irresponsible to relying on one opinion or perspective in any scientific endeavor, especially a topic with the social relevance of crime and responses to crime. The apparent correspondence between police recording and victim reporting of serious violent crimes teaches us that crime is not directly observable and the manner in which we measure crime *changes* over time. This is not unimportant.

Under ideal conditions the best indicators remain proxy measures at best, variable factors that transform resulting from organizational and administrative changes, social perceptions of crime, and most importantly, the responses of individuals- police, victims, and the public. An interesting question to consider is whether official statistics might have changed without knowledge of the nature and extent of crime as reflected in the NCVS. We do not know whether police recording practices might have changed without the presence of a secondary measure. Additionally, a second measure of crime does much in the eyes of the public to legitimize the picture of crime generated by law enforcement. The essence of these sentiments is

captured well by Josiah Stamp (1929:258) who offered this anecdote
regarding official statistics:

> The individual source of the statistics may easily be the
> weakest link. Harold Cox tells a story of his life as a young
> man in India. He quoted some statistics to a Judge, an
> Englishman, and a very good fellow. His friend said, "Cox,
> when you are a bit older, you will not quote Indian statistics
> with that assurance. The Government are very keen on
> amassing statistics— they collect them, add them, raise them
> to the nth power, take the cube root and prepare wonderful
> diagrams. But what you must never forget is that every one of
> these figures comes in the first place from the *chowty dar*
> [village watchman], who just puts down whatever he damn
> pleases."

Endnotes

Chapter 1

1. In the discussion that follows, NCVS is used to denote both the NCS and NCVS from 1973 until present.

2. After briefly converging, the two series have now diverged once more. The relationship may therefore be described as a correspondence or congruence between the two series. These terms are used interchangeably throughout the book.

Chapter 2

1. The exact number of actual police agencies in the United States is unknown so an exact number of agencies represented by the UCR program is an approximation (Maguire, 2002).

Chapter 3

1. O'Brien (1999b) suggests using a Dickey-Fuller test between male and female UCR crime counts to test whether convergence between two series meets the statistical criteria for convergence. LaFree and Drass (2002) use a similar approach in their examination of whether homicide rates across countries are converging and diverging. This study does not use a formal test of cointegration as do the previous two studies. Rather, the increasing correspondence between the NCVS and UCR is characterized by a "crossing over" of the two series. In absolute numbers at least, the two series have apparently converged and are diverging once more.

2. Individual response rates are calculated from households that agree to participate in the survey. Therefore personal response rates may be higher during a given year depending on the number of individuals residing within the average household on an annual basis.

Chapter 5

1. 911 usage may be considered an innovation in policing, and thus according to Rogers (1995) be modeled as an s shaped curve characterized by a "tipping point" after which time a trend will increase exponentially. For the present study, implementation of 911 was modeled using linear interpolation rather than as a growth or diffusion function.

2. The two variables "not okay to strike" and "the courts are harsh enough" were reverse coded so as to be in a positive response format like the other GSS variables.

3. These results are available from the author upon request.

Chapter 6

1. The results for serious violent crime are not presented here but are available from the author upon request.

2. The negative relationship between NCVS technology and NCVS rape counts is most likely spurious, best described as an example of "correlation does not equal causation."

Appendices 1-7

ANALYSIS OF THE CONVERGENCE BETWEEN VICTIM REPORTING AND POLICE RECORDING OF SERIOUS VIOLENT CRIME, 1973-2002

APPENDIX 1

Graphs of Individual Variables Used in the Analysis of the Convergence Between Victim Reporting and Police Recording of Serious Violent Crime, 1973-2002

Note: All data points calculated by interpolation are marked.

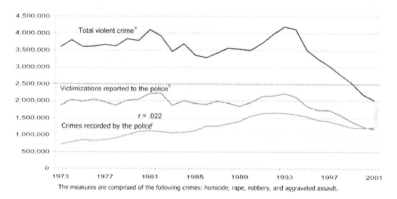

Graph 1. Measures of Serious Violent Crime, 1973-2002.
Source: [a,b]National Crime Victimization Survey and [b]Uniform Crime Report.

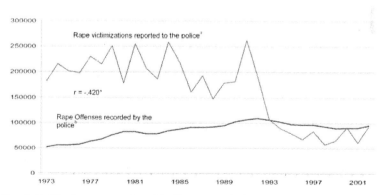

Graph 2. Victim-reported and Police-recorded Rape, 1973-2002.
Source: [a,b]National Crime Victimization Survey and [b]Uniform Crime Report.

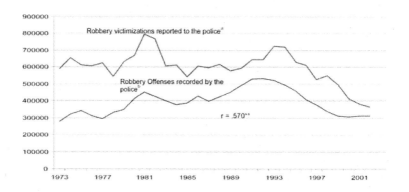

Graph 3. Victim-reported and Police-recorded robbery, 1973-2002.
Source: [a,b]National Crime Victimization Survey and [b]Uniform
Crime Report.

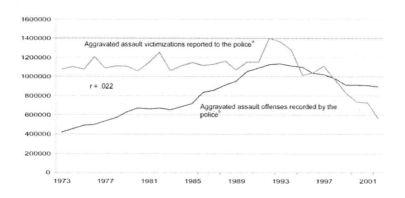

Graph 4. Victim-reported and Police-recorded Aggravated Assault,
1973-2002.
Source: [a,b]National Crime Victimization Survey and [b]Uniform
Crime Report.

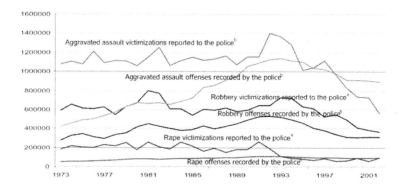

Graph 5. All Reported and Recorded Serious Violent Crime, 1973-
2002.
Source: [a,b]National Crime Victimization Survey and [b]Uniform
Crime Report.

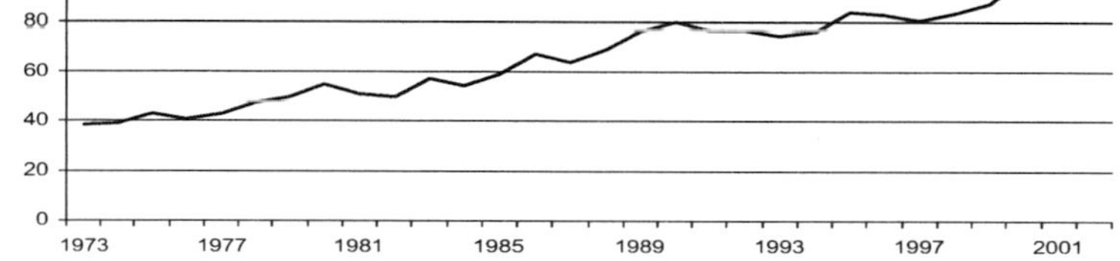

Graph 6. Serious Violent Crime, 1973-2002. The variable is generated
as the UCR count divided by the NCVS count multiplied by
100.
Source: [a,b]National Crime Victimization Survey and [b]Uniform
Crime Report.

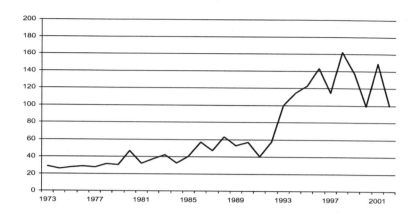

Graph 7. Rape, 1973-2002. The variable is generated as the UCR count
divided by the NCVS count multiplied by 100.
Source: [a,b]National Crime Victimization Survey and [b]Uniform
Crime Report.

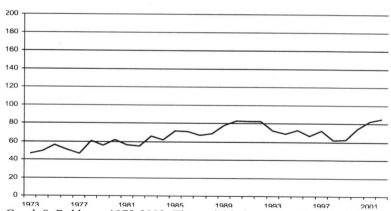

Graph 8. Robbery, 1973-2002. The variable is generated as the UCR
count divided by the NCVS count multiplied by 100.
Source: [a,b]National Crime Victimization Survey and [b]Uniform
Crime Report.

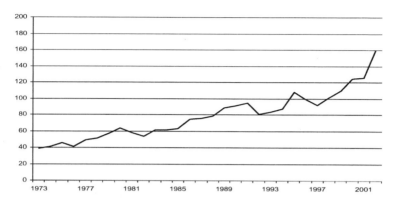

Graph 9. Aggravated Assault, 1973-2002. The variable is generated as
the UCR count divided by the NCVS count multiplied by 100.
Source: [a,b]National Crime Victimization Survey and [b]Uniform
Crime Report.

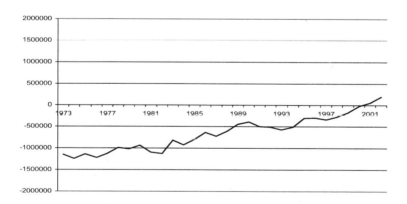

Graph 10. Difference Scores for Serious Violent Crime, 1973-2002.
The variable is generated as the UCR count subtracted from
the NCVS count.
Source: [a,b]National Crime Victimization Survey and [b]Uniform
Crime Report.

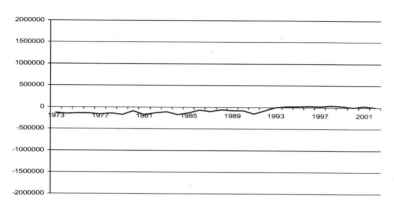

Graph 11. Difference Score for Rape, 1973-2002. The variable is
generated as the UCR count subtracted from the NCVS count.
Source: [a,b]National Crime Victimization Survey and [b]Uniform
Crime Report.

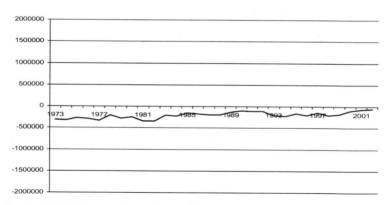

Graph 12. Difference Score for Robbery, 1973-2002. The variable is
generated as the UCR count subtracted from the NCVS count.
Source: [a,b]National Crime Victimization Survey and [b]Uniform
Crime Report.

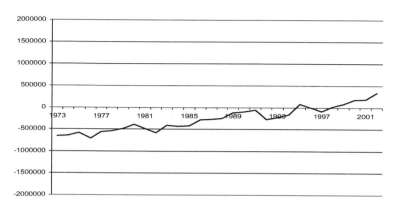

Graph 13. Difference Score for Aggravated Assault, 1973-2002. The variable is generated as the UCR count subtracted from the NCVS count.
Source: [a,b]National Crime Victimization Survey and [b]Uniform Crime Report.

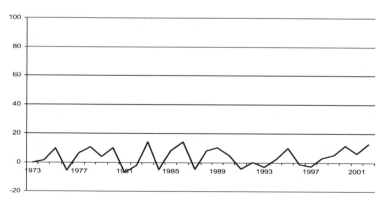

Graph 14. Percent Change Score for Serious Violent Crime, 1973-2002.
Source: [a,b]National Crime Victimization Survey and [b]Uniform Crime Report.

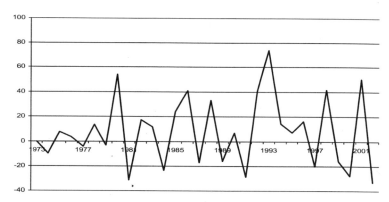

Graph 15. Percent Change Score for Rape, 1973-2002. The variable is
constructed as (UCR/NCVS)*100.
Source: [a,b]National Crime Victimization Survey and [b]Uniform
Crime Report.

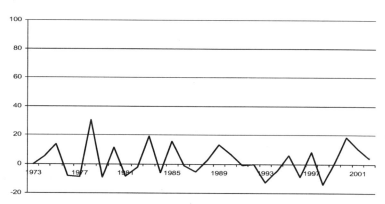

Graph 16. Percent Change Score for Robbery, 1973-2002. The variable
is constructed as (UCR/NCVS)*100.
Source: [a,b]National Crime Victimization Survey and [b]Uniform
Crime Report.

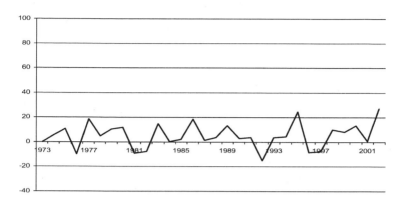

Graph G17. Percent Change Score for Aggravated Assault. The
variable is constructed as (UCR/NCVS)*100.
Source: [a,b]National Crime Victimization Survey and [b]Uniform
Crime Report.

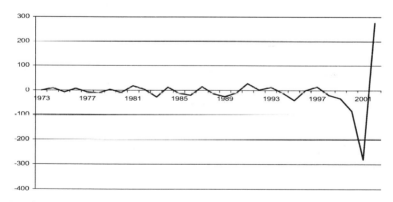

Graph 18. Percent Change Score for Serious Violent Crime, 1973-
2002. The dependent variable is constructed as (UCR-
NCVS)*100.
Source: [a,b]National Crime Victimization Survey and [b]Uniform
Crime Report.

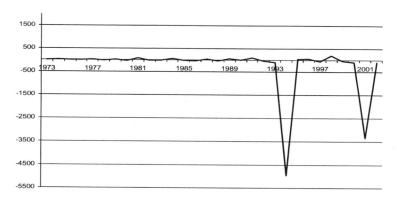

Graph 19. Percent Change Score for Rape, 1973-2002. The dependent
variable is constructed as (UCR-NCVS)*100.
Source: [a,b]National Crime Victimization Survey and [b]Uniform
Crime Report.

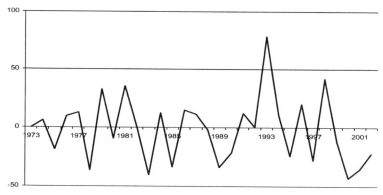

Graph 20. Percent Change for Robbery, 1973-2002. The dependent
variable is constructed as (UCR-NCVS)*100.
Source: [a,b]National Crime Victimization Survey and [b]Uniform
Crime Report.

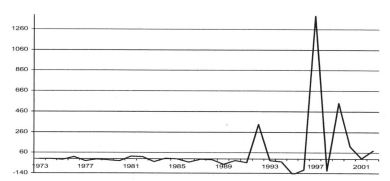

Graph 21. Percent Change Score for Aggravated Assault, 1973-2002.
The dependent variable is constructed as (UCR-NCVS)*100.
Source: [a,b]National Crime Victimization Survey and [b]Uniform
Crime Report.

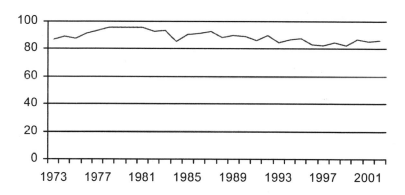

Graph 22. Actual percent of population covered by UCR (agencies
reporting 12 months).
Source: Crime in the United States, 1973-2002.

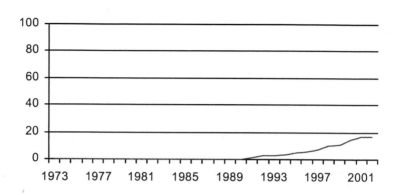

Graph 23. Percent of population covered by NIBRS.
Source: Bureau of Justice Statistics.

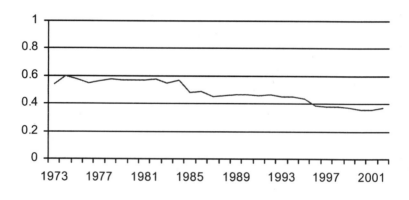

Graph 24. Arrest ratio of aggravated to simple assault.
Source: Crime in the United States, 1973-2002.

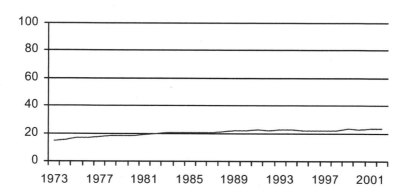

Graph 25. Percent civilian employees in cities.
Source: Crime in the United States, 1973-2002.

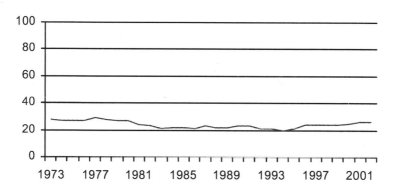

Graph 26. Percent commercial robbery.
Source: Crime in the United States, 1973-2002.

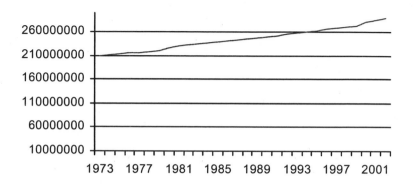

Graph 27. UCR population base.
  Source: Crime in the United States, 1973-2002.

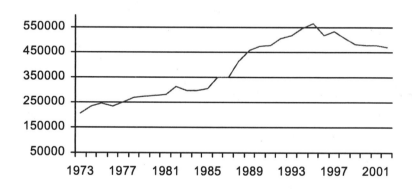

Graph 28. Number of aggravated assault arrests.
  Source: Crime in the United States, 1973-2002.

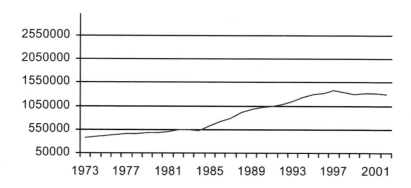

Graph 29. Number of simple assault arrests.
Source: Crime in the United States, 1973-2002.

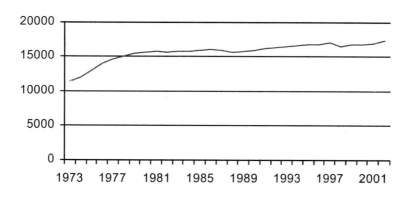

Graph 30. Total agencies reporting under UCR.
Source: Crime in the United States, 1973-2002.

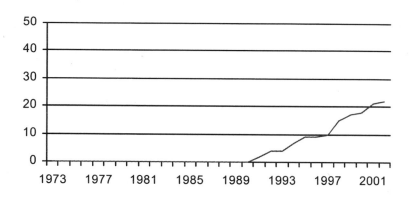

Graph 31. Number of states testing or certified NIBRS.
Source: NIBRS data files, 1990-2002.

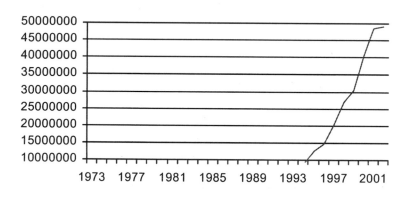

Graph 32. Population covered by NIBRS.
Source: NIBRS data files, 1990-2002.

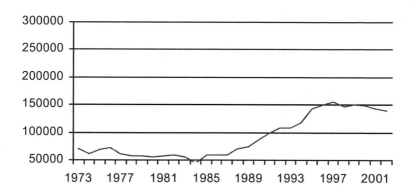

Graph 33. Number of arrests for offenses against family and children.
Source: Crime in the United States, 1973-2002.

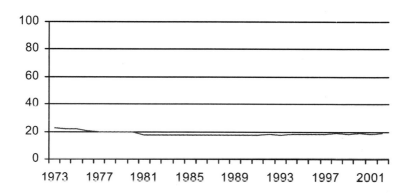

Graph 34. Percent of the U.S. population under 12 years of age.
Source: Criminal Victimization in the United States and U.S.
Department of Census.

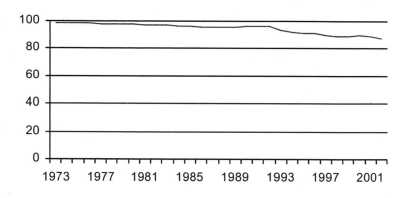

Graph 35. NCVS person response rate.
   Source: Criminal Victimization in the United States, 1973-
   2002.

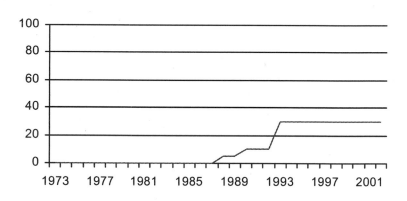

Graph 36. Percent CATI interviews.
   Source: Criminal Victimization in the United States, 1973-
   2002.

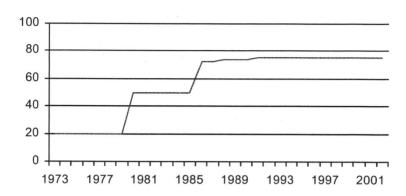

Graph 37. Percent telephone interviews.
Source: Criminal Victimization in the United States, 1973-2002.

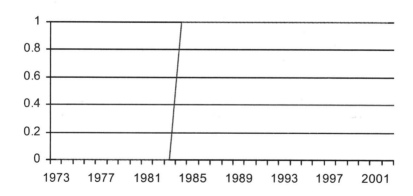

Graph 38. Primary sampling unit reduction.
Source: Criminal Victimization in the United States 1973-2002.

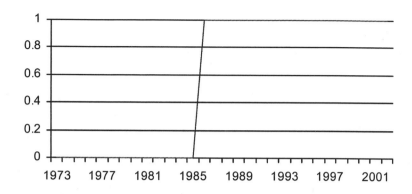

Graph 39. Change in proxy interviews.
    Source: Criminal Victimization in the United States, 1973-
    2002.

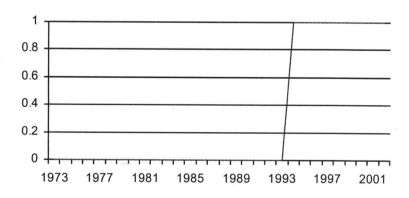

Graph 40. NCVS redesign.
    Source: Criminal Victimization in the United States, 1973-
    2002.

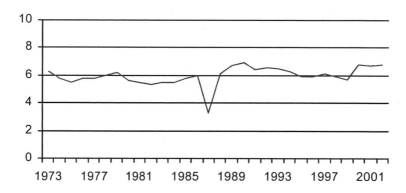

Graph 41. Percent unbounded interviews.
Source: Criminal Victimization in the United States, 1973-
2002.

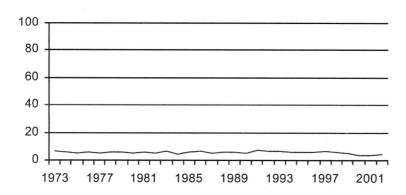

Graph 42. Percent of total serious violent crime that are series offenses.
Source: Criminal Victimization in the United States, 1973-
2002.

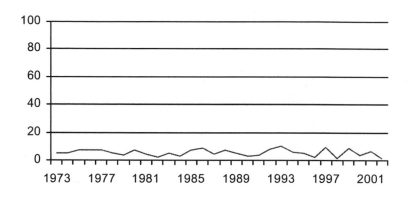

Graph 43. Percent of total rapes that are series offenses.
        Source: Criminal Victimization in the United States, 1973-
        2002.

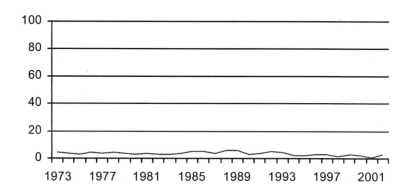

Graph 44. Percent of total robberies that are series offenses.
        Source: Criminal Victimization in the United States, 1973-
        2002.

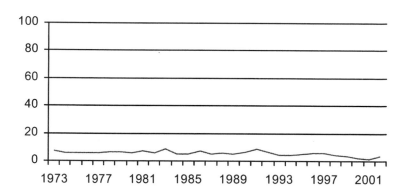

Graph 45. Percent of total aggravated assaults that are series offenses.
Source: Criminal Victimization in the United States, 1973-
2002.

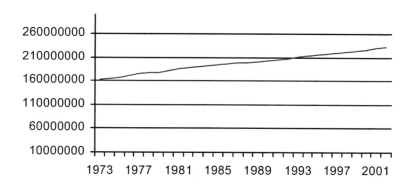

Graph 46. NCVS population base 12+ years of age.
Source: Criminal Victimization in the United States, 1973-
2002.

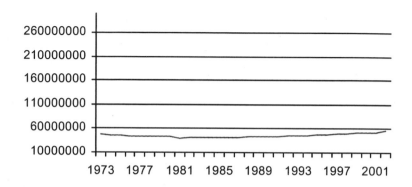

Graph 47. Total population under 12 years of age.
    Source: Criminal Victimization in the United States, 1973-
    2002.

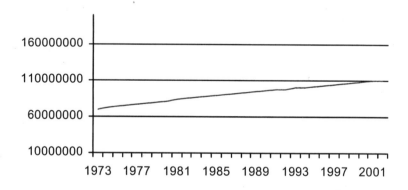

Graph 48. NCVS household population base.
    Source: Criminal Victimization in the United States, 1973-
    2002.

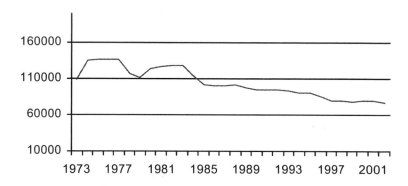

Graph 49. Number of persons interviewed.
  Source: Criminal Victimization in the United States, 1973-
  2002.

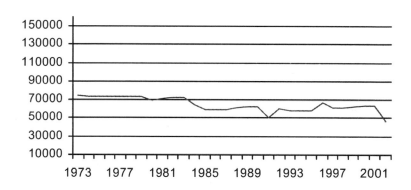

Graph 50. Number of sampled households.
  Source: Criminal Victimization in the United States, 1973-
  2002.

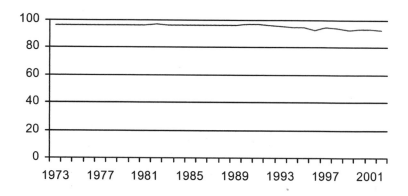

Graph 51. Household response rate.
    Source: Criminal Victimization in the United States, 1973-
    2002.

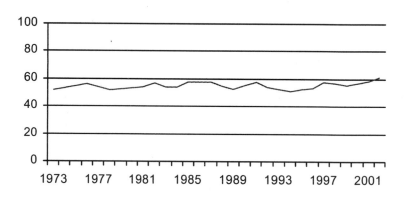

Graph 52. Percent of serious violent crime reported to police.
    Source: Criminal Victimization in the United States, 1973-
    2002.

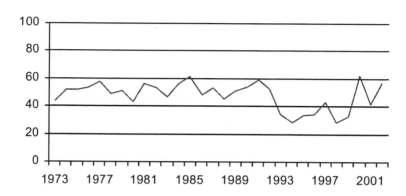

Graph 53. Percent of rape reported to the police.
 Source: Criminal Victimization in the United States, 1973-
 2002.

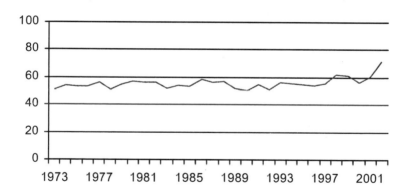

Graph 54. Percent of robbery reported to the police.
 Source: Criminal Victimization in the United States, 1973-
 2002.

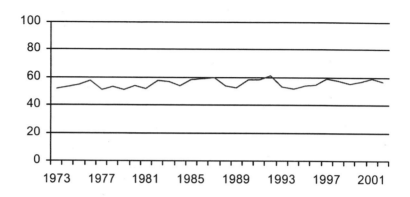

Graph 55. Percent of aggravated assault reported to the police.
Source: Criminal Victimization in the United States, 1973-
2002.

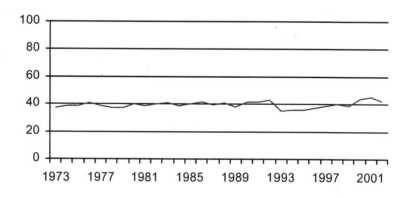

Graph 56. Percent of simple assaults reported to the police.
Source: Criminal Victimization in the United States, 1973-
2002.

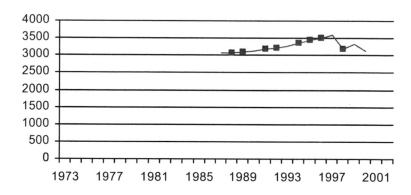

Graph 57. Total sampling frame for LEMAS.
Source: LEMAS, Bureau of Justice Statistics, 1987-2000.

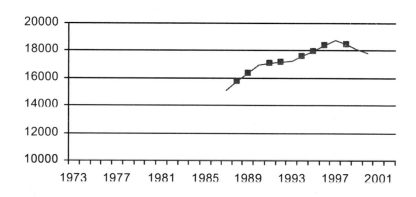

Graph 58. Agency total weighted.
Source: LEMAS, Bureau of Justice Statistics, 1987-2000.

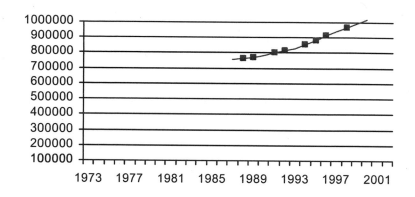

Graph 59. Officer total weighted.
    Source: LEMAS, Bureau of Justice Statistics, 1987-2000.

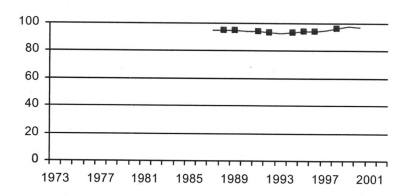

Graph 60. LEMAS response rate.
    Source: LEMAS, Bureau of Justice Statistics, 1987-2000.

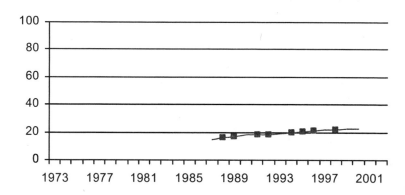

Graph 61. Percent minority officers.
    Source: LEMAS, Bureau of Justice Statistics, 1987-2000.

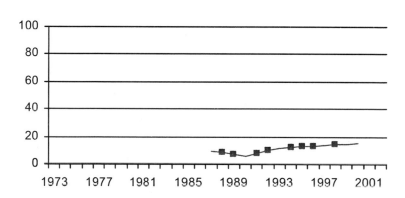

Graph 62. Departments requiring an educational requirement.
    Source: LEMAS, Bureau of Justice Statistics, 1987-2000.

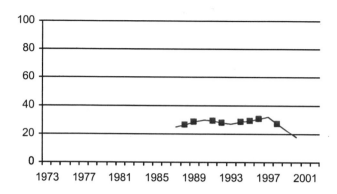

Graph 63. Basic 911 participation.
Source: LEMAS, Bureau of Justice Statistics, 1987-2000.

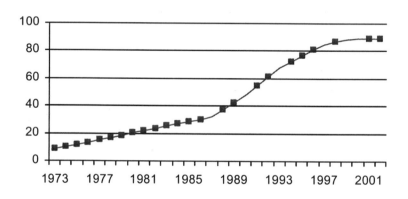

Graph 64. 911 participation.
Source: LEMAS, Congressional Record, May 1999.

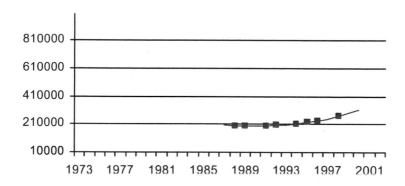

Graph 65. Total civilians in workforce.
Source: LEMAS, Bureau of Justice Statistics, 1987-2000.

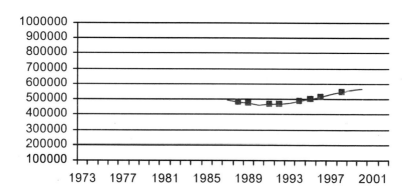

Graph 66. Local police department total officers weighted.
Source: LEMAS, Bureau of Justice Statistics, 1987-2000.

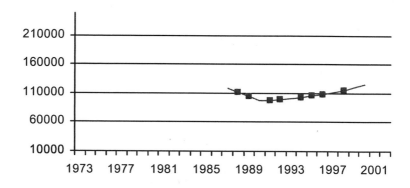

Graph 67. Local police department total civilian workers weighted.
Source: LEMAS, Bureau of Justice Statistics, 1987-2000.

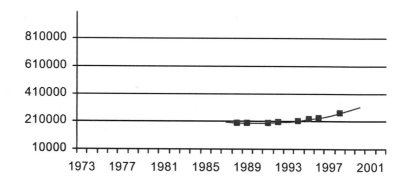

Graph 68. Total civilians in local agency workforce.
Source: LEMAS, Bureau of Justice Statistics, 1987-2000.

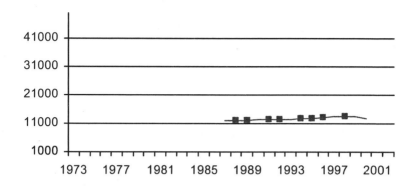

Graph 69. Number of local police departments weighted.
Source: LEMAS, Bureau of Justice Statistics, 1987-2000.

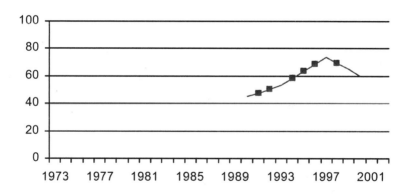

Graph 70. Percent using computers for record keeping.
Source: LEMAS, Bureau of Justice Statistics, 1990-2000.

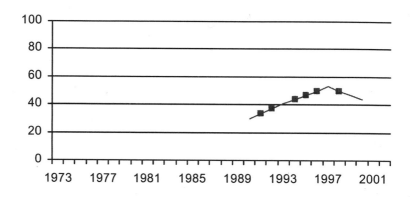

Graph 71. Percent using computers for criminal investigation.
Source: LEMAS, Bureau of Justice Statistics, 1990-2000.

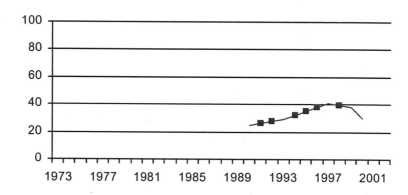

Graph 72. Percent using computers for crime analysis.
Source: LEMAS, Bureau of Justice Statistics, 1990-2000.

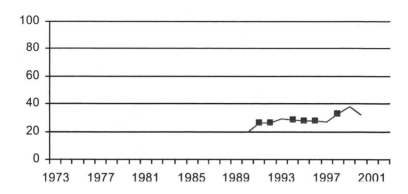

Graph 73. Percent using computers for dispatch.
     Source: LEMAS, Bureau of Justice Statistics, 1990-2000.

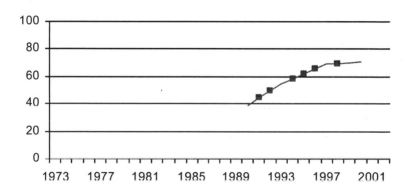

Graph 74. Percent using computers for arrests.
     Source: LEMAS, Bureau of Justice Statistics, 1990-2000.

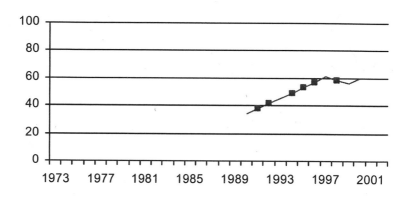

Graph 75. Percent with in field calls for service access.
Source: LEMAS, Bureau of Justice Statistics, 1990-2000.

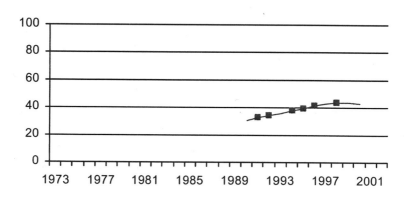

Graph 76. Percent using computers for warrants.
Source: LEMAS, Bureau of Justice Statistics, 1990-2000.

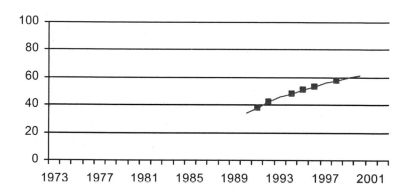

Graph 77. Percent using computers to file traffic warrants.
Source: LEMAS, Bureau of Justice Statistics, 1990-2000.

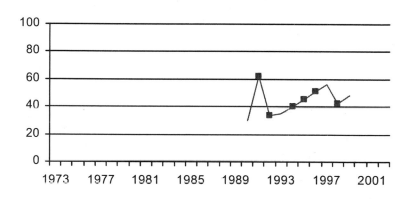

Graph 78. Percent using computers for UCR file management.
Source: LEMAS, Bureau of Justice Statistics, 1990-2000.

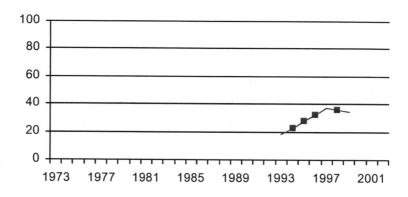

Graph 79. Percent using computers for NIBRS file management.
Source: LEMAS, Bureau of Justice Statistics, 1993-1999.

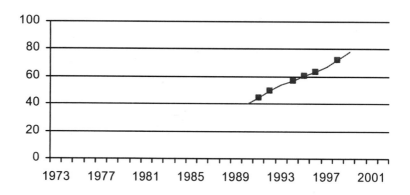

Graph 80. Percent using personal computers.
Source: LEMAS, Bureau of Justice Statistics, 1990-1999.

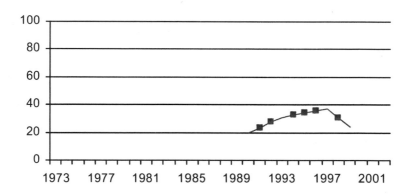

Graph 81. Percent using mainframe computers.
    Source: LEMAS, Bureau of Justice Statistics, 1990-1999.

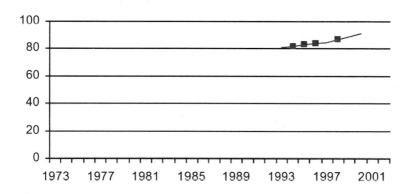

Graph 82. Percent with written policies regarding domestic violence.
    Source: LEMAS, Bureau of Justice Statistics, 1993-2000.

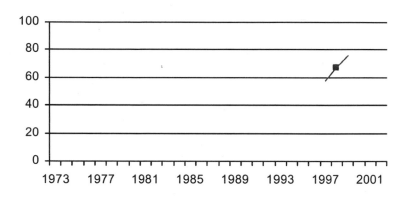

Graph 83. Percent with written policies regarding citizen complaints.
Source: LEMAS, Bureau of Justice Statistics, 1993-1997.

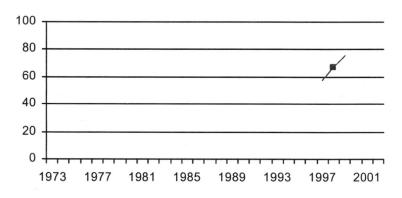

Graph 84. Percent with written policies regarding discretionary arrest.
Source: LEMAS, Bureau of Justice Statistics, 1993-1997.

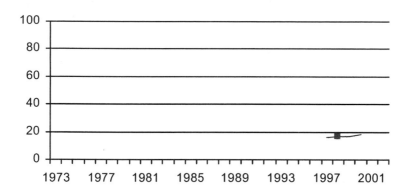

Graph 85. Percent with formal COPS program.
    Source: LEMAS, Bureau of Justice Statistics, 1997-2000.

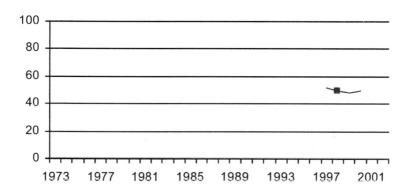

Graph 86. Percent with informal COPS program.
    Source: LEMAS, Bureau of Justice Statistics, 1997-2000.

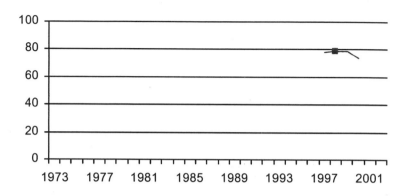

Graph 87. Percent with community meetings.
Source: LEMAS, Bureau of Justice Statistics, 1997-2000.

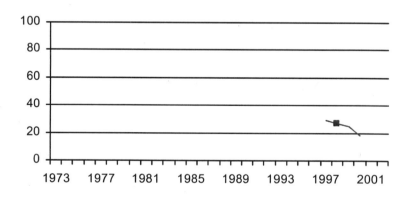

Graph 88. Percent engaging in problem solving with community.
Source: LEMAS, Bureau of Justice Statistics, 1997-2000.

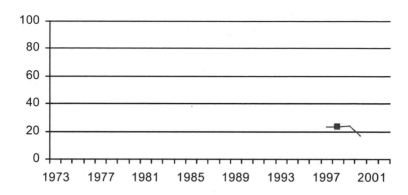

Graph 89. Percent with citizen training.
Source: LEMAS, Bureau of Justice Statistics, 1997-2000.

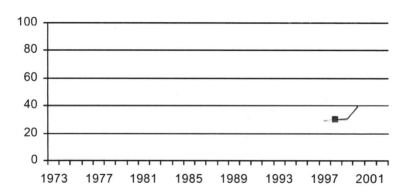

Graph 90. Percent with field computers.
Source: LEMAS, Bureau of Justice Statistics, 1997-2000.

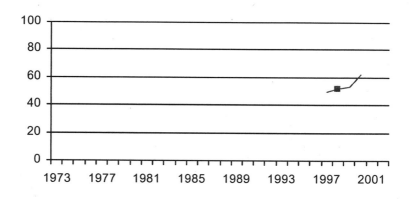

Graph 91. Percent utilizing foot patrol.
Source: LEMAS, Bureau of Justice Statistics, 1997-2000.

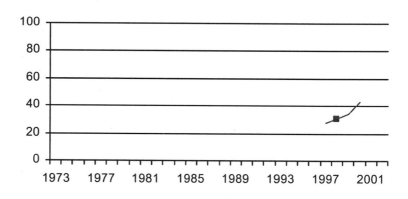

Graph 92. Percent utilizing bike patrol.
Source: LEMAS, Bureau of Justice Statistics, 1997-2000.

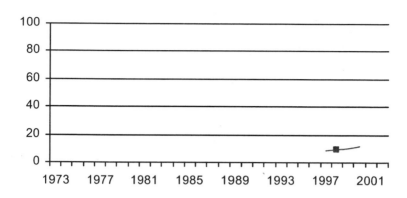

Graph 93. Percent utilizing motorcycle patrol.
    Source: LEMAS, Bureau of Justice Statistics, 1997-2000.

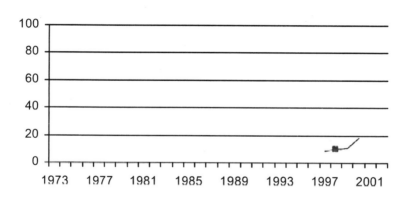

Graph 94. Percent with in field calls for service access.
    Source: LEMAS, Bureau of Justice Statistics, 1997-2000.

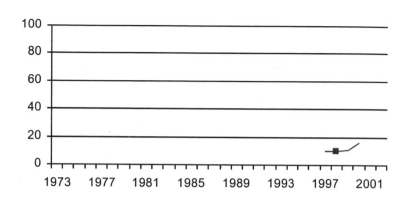

Graph 95. Percent with in field criminal history access.
Source: LEMAS, Bureau of Justice Statistics, 1997-2000.

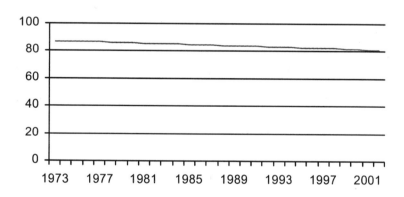

Graph 96. Percent of U.S. males that are white.
Source: United States Department of Census, 1973-2002.

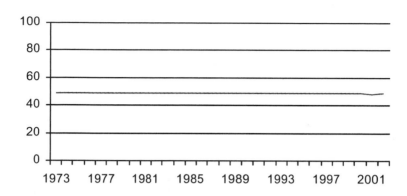

Graph 97. Percent of U.S. population that is male.
Source: United States Department of Census, 1973-2002.

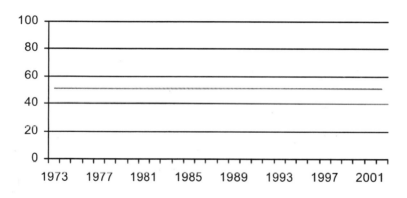

Graph 98. Percent of U.S. population that is female.
Source: United States Department of Census, 1973-2002.

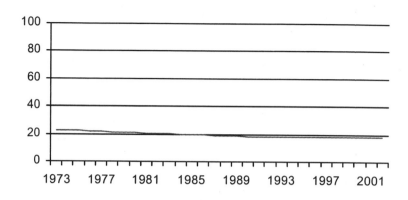

Graph 99. Percent of U.S. male population under the age of 24.
Source: United States Department of Census, 1973-2002.

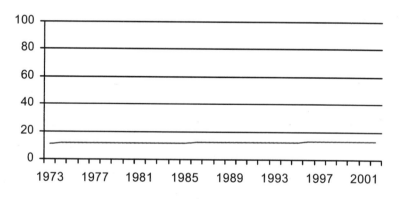

Graph 100. Percent of U.S. population that is Black.
Source: United States Department of Census, 1973-2002.

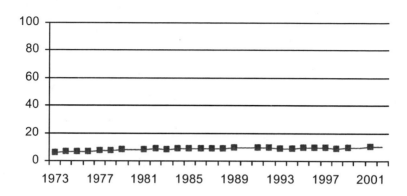

Graph 101. Percent of U.S. population that is single.
Source: United States Department of Census, 1973-2002.

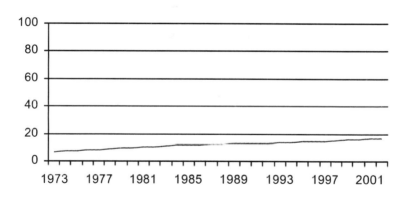

Graph 102. Percent of U.S. population with 4 or more years higher
education.
Source: United States Department of Census, 1973-2002.

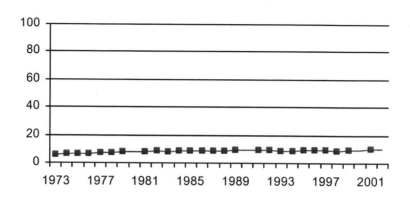

Graph 103. Percent of U.S. population living alone.
          Source: United States Department of Census, 1973-2002.

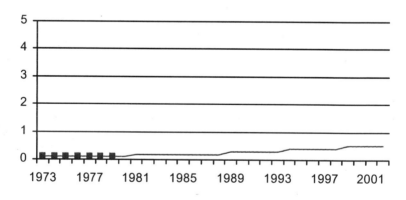

Graph 104. Percent of U.S. population in prison.
          Source: Bureau of Justice Statistics, 1973-2002.

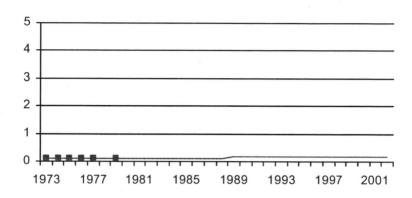

Graph 105. Percent of U.S. population in Jail.
Source: Bureau of Justice Statistics, 1973-2002.

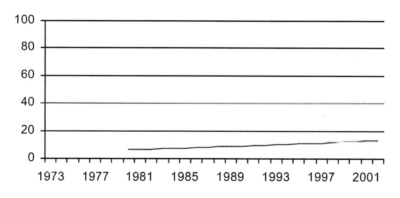

Graph 106. Percent of U.S. population that is Hispanic.
Source: United States Department of Census, 1980-2002.

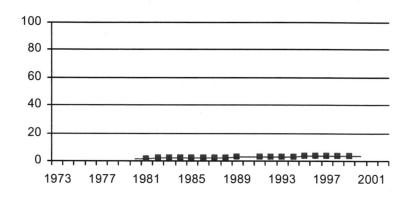

Graph 107. Percent of U.S. population speaking English not well/not at all.
Source: United States Department of Census, 1980-2000.

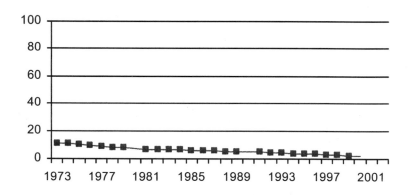

Graph 108. Percent of U.S. population with no telephone.
Source: United States Department of Census, 1980-2000.

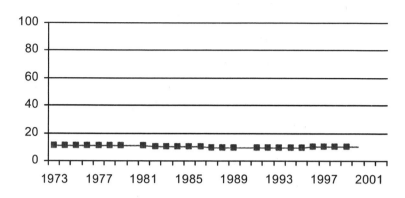

Graph 109. Percent of U.S. homeowners moving in the last year.
Source: United States Department of Census, 1980-2000.

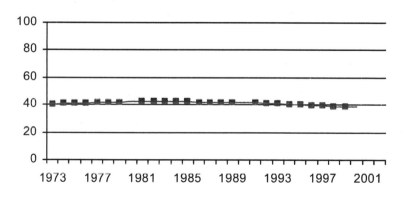

Graph 110. Percent of U.S. renters moving in the last year.
Source: United States Department of Census, 1980-2000.

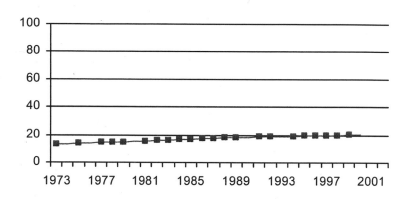

Graph 111. Percent of U.S. homeowners that live alone.
Source: United States Department of Census, 1980-2000.

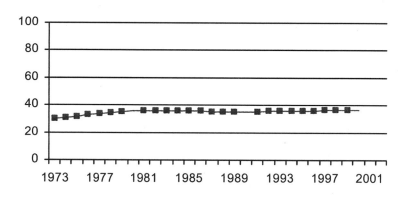

Graph 112. Percent of U.S. renters that live alone.
Source: United States Department of Census, 1980-2000.

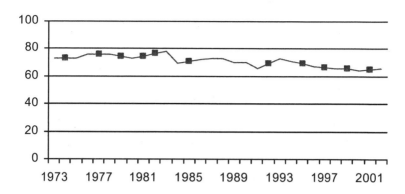

Graph 113. Percent that imagine a situation where police may strike an
  adult male citizen.
  Source: General Social Survey, 1973-2002.

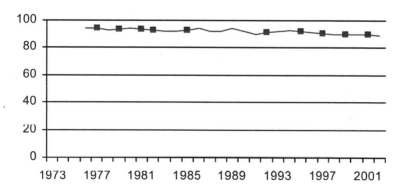

Graph 114. Percent approving of police striking a citizen when
  attacked.
  Source: General Social Survey, 1976-2002.

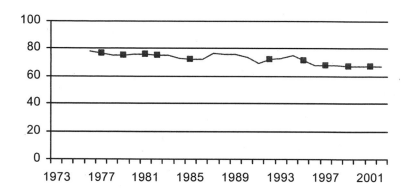

Graph 115. Percent approving of police striking a citizen for trying to
escape.
Source: General Social Survey, 1976-2002.

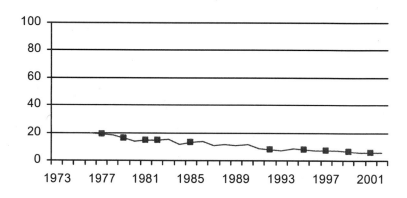

Graph 116. Percent approving of police striking a citizen for using
vulgar language.
Source: General Social Survey, 1976-2002.

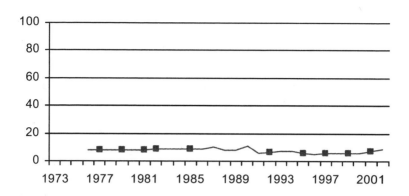

Graph 117. Percent approving of police striking a suspect in a murder
   investigation.
   Source: General Social Survey, 1976-2002.

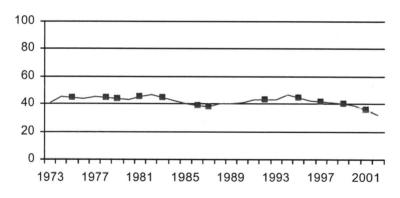

Graph 118. GSS: Percent stating they are afraid to walk alone at night
   in their neighborhood.
   Source: General Social Survey, 1973-2002.

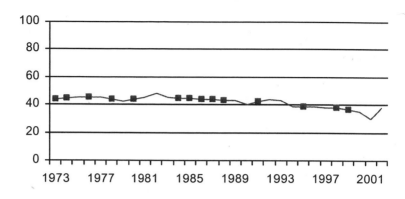

Graph 119. Gallup poll: Percent stating they are afraid to walk alone at
     night.
     Source: Gallup Poll, 1973-2002.

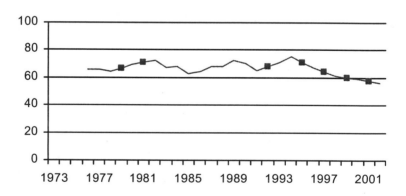

Graph 120. Percent stating too little money is spent on crime control.
     Source: General Social Survey, 1976-2002.

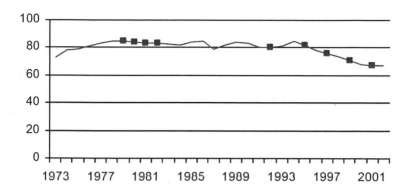

Graph 121. Percent stating courts are not harsh enough with criminals.
Source: General Social Survey, 1973-2002.

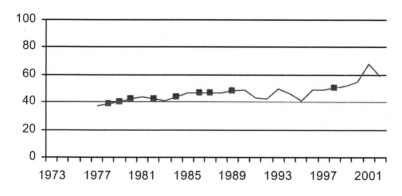

Graph 122. Percent stating ethics of police are very high/high.
Source: General Social Survey, 1976-2002.

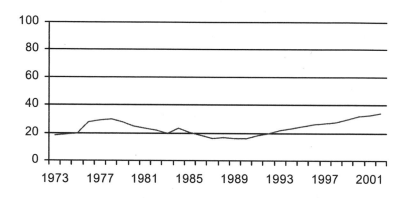

Graph 123. Percent approving legalization of marijuana.
Source: General Social Survey, 1973-2002.

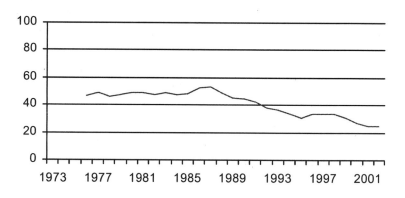

Graph 124. Percent agreeing laws against homosexual relationships are
    important.
    Source: General Social Survey, 1976-2002.

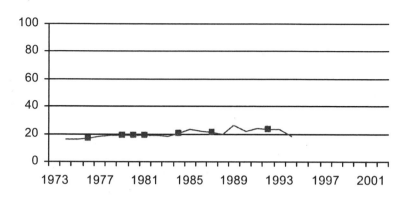

Graph 125. Percent approve of wiretapping.
    Source: General Social Survey, 1974-1994.

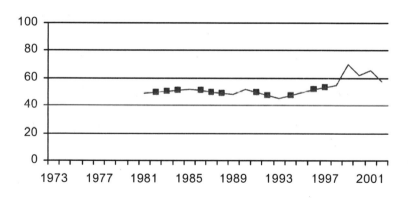

Graph 126. Confidence in police to protect.
    Source: General Social Survey, 1981-1994.

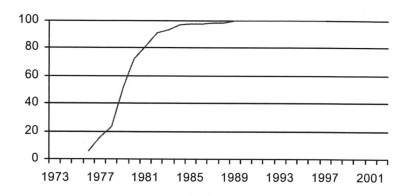

Graph 127. Any protection from abuse legislation, 1976-1997.
Source: Dugan, Nagin, and Rosenfeld, 2003.

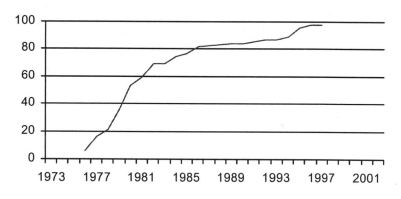

Graph 128. No contact protection order, 1976-1997.
Source: Dugan, Nagin, and Rosenfeld, 2003.

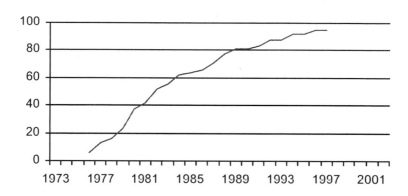

Graph 129. Eligibility beyond cohabitation, 1976-1997.
Source: Dugan, Nagin, and Rosenfeld, 2003.

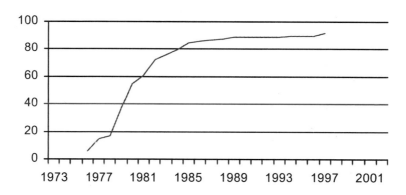

Graph 130. Victim custody relief, 1976-1997.
Source: Dugan, Nagin, and Rosenfeld, 2003.

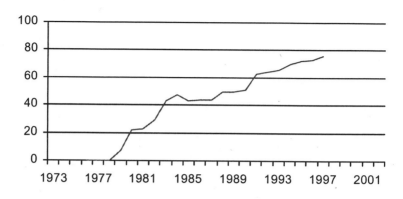

Graph 131. Misdemeanor for violating protection order, 1976-1997.
Source: Dugan, Nagin, and Rosenfeld, 2003.

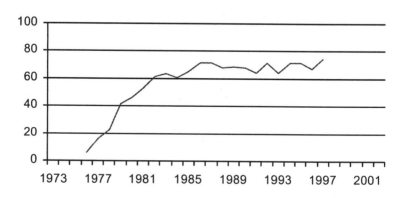

Graph 132. Civil or criminal contempt, 1976-1997.
Source: Dugan, Nagin, and Rosenfeld, 2003.

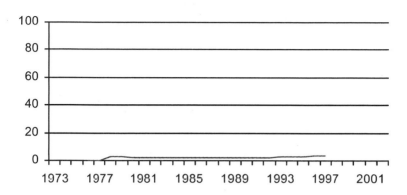

Graph 133. Felony for protection order violation, 1976-1997.
Source: Dugan, Nagin, and Rosenfeld, 2003.

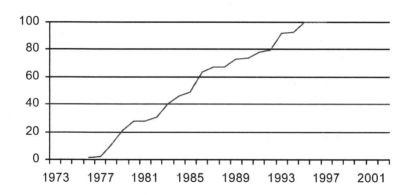

Graph 134. Warrantless arrest is okay, 1976-1997.
Source: Dugan, Nagin, and Rosenfeld, 2003.

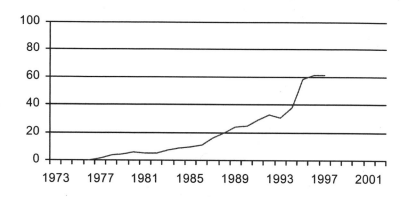

Graph 135. Mandatory arrest for protection order violation, 1976-1997.
Source: Dugan, Nagin, and Rosenfeld, 2003.

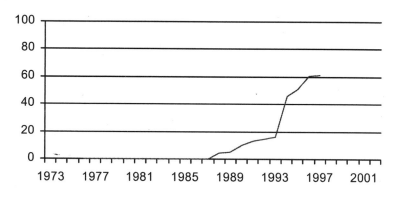

Graph 136. Firearm confiscation for protection order violation, 1976-1997.
Source: Dugan, Nagin, and Rosenfeld, 2003.

APPENDIX 2

Chronology and summary of major design changes in the National Crime Victimization Survey over time, 1973-2002

Year	Design Change
Mid-1960s	The first U.S. victimization surveys are carried out by the National Opinion Research Center for the President's Commission on Law Enforcement and Administration.
	Task Force Report: Crime and Its Impact- An Assessment. Washington, USGPO, 1967; Biderman, Johnson, McIntyre, and Weir, *Report on a Pilot Study in the District of Columbia on Victimization and Attitudes Toward Law Enforcement,* Field Studies I, President's Commission on Law Enforcement and Administration of Justice. Washington: USGPO 1967; Ennis, *Criminal Victimization in the United States: A Report of a National Survey.* Field Studies II, President's Commission on Law Enforcement and Administration of Justice, Washington: USGPO, 1967.
1967-1968	The Census Bureau conference on the need for law enforcement, courts, and corrections data.
	U.S. Department of Commerce, Bureau of the Census, *Report on National Needs for Criminal Justice Statistics,* Washington: USGPO, 1968.
1969	The Statistics Division is organized in the Law Enforcement Assistance Administration (LEAA). Planning for the National Crime Survey begins.
1970	The first reverse record check study is conducted in Washington, D.C. Known victims (identified through police records) were interviewed to test the questionnaire.
1970	Baltimore reverse record check study.
1971	San Jose reverse record check study.
	San Jose Methods Test of Known Crime Victims. Washington: Law Enforcement Assistance Administration (LEAA), 1972.

Year	Design Change
1971	Household victimization surveys in San Jose and Dayton, using probability sample. *Crime and Victims: A Report on the Dayton-San Jose Pilot Survey of Victimization.* Law Enforcement Assistance Administration, National Criminal Justice Information and Statistics Service. Washington: June, 1974.
	First and second victimization supplements to Quarterly Household Survey (QHS). Designed to indicate sample size needed for reliable estimates of victimization and to resolve remaining methodological issues.
1972	Third and final QHS supplements.
July 1973	Data collection for NCS sample begins. Half of sample introduced during this period. A rotating panel design is adopted that requires seven successive interviews at 6-month interval for all eligible respondents at a housing location.
	Commercial Victimization Survey begins.
	First Cities Surveys conducted in eight impact cities: Atlanta, Baltimore, Cleveland, Dallas, Denver, Newark, Portland OR, and St. Louis.
1973	Remainder of national sample introduced to produce a total of 72, 000 housing locations in active sample.
	Cities surveys conducted in large urban centers: Chicago, Detroit, Los Angeles, New York, and Philadelphia.
	All NCS interviews are conducted in person. Interviews 2-7 are administered in the same manner as the original interview
1974	One-time cities surveys conducted in Boston, Buffalo, Cincinnati, Houston, Miami, Milwaukee, Minneapolis, New Orleans, Oakland, Pittsburgh, San Diego, San Francisco. and Washington, D.C.
1974-76	National Academy of Sciences reviews NCS program.
	Surveying Crime, Penick and Owens, ed. Washington: National Academy of Sciences, 1976.

Year	Design Change
1975	Cities surveys replicated in impact cities and large urban centers.
1976	NCS national sample matures. In-rotation of new sample unit fully balanced by out-rotation sample scheduled for all 7 interviews. Provides full comparability of annual estimates.
	Criminal Victimization in the United States, 1973 is released. This is the first report based on the nation NCS sample.
1976-77	The Bureau of the Census experiments on the effect of personal visits versus telephone interviews.
	Woltman and Bushery, *Results of the NCS Maximum Personal Visit- Maximum Telephone Interview Experiment.* Washington: U.S. Bureau of the Census, Statistical Methods Division, 1977.
1977	Congressional hearings on continuation of the NCS program. As a result of the Nation Academy Evaluation, LEAA considered suspending data collection, pending outcome of research and design project to redesign the survey. House Subcommittee on Crime examined implications of this proposal.
	Hearing before the Subcommittee on Crime of the Committee on the Judiciary, House of Representatives, Ninety-Fifth congress, First Session on Suspension of the National Crime Survey, October 13, 1977, Serial No. 23. Washington: USGPO, 1977.
	Commercial Victimization Survey (CVS) is suspended, because of two concerns: (1) FBI's Uniform Crime Reports collected such data well, and CVS appeared to duplicate this function; (2) obstacles to maintaining current sampling frame for commercial victims limited the accuracy of and utility of CVS estimates.

Year	Design Change
1978	LEAA Statistics Division sponsors conference in Leesburg, VA to evaluate NCS conceptual and methodological issues.
	A total sample of 73,000 is chosen for the survey. A sub-sample of 8,000 housing units were administered a special questionnaire for research purposes. The remaining 65,000 housing units were used to generate victimization estimates for 1978.
	Request for proposals issued for major redesign of NCS.
1979	Modifications to NCS-2 (incident form) are introduced.
	NCS redesign contract awarded to Crime Survey Research Consortium (CSRC), headed by the Bureau of Social Science Research (BSSR).
1979	New crime legislation splits LEAA into separate program agencies, among them the Bureau of Justice Statistics (BJS), which assumes responsibility for NCS.
	A total sample of 73,000 is chosen for the survey. A sub-sample of 12,000 housing units were administered a special questionnaire for research purposes. The remaining 62,000 housing units were used to generate victimization estimates for 1979.
1980	Proportion of NCS phone interviews is increased from 20% to 50%. Telephone interviewing is increased to cut costs of implementing the survey. Approximately 50% of all interviews are now done telephone. Interviews 1,3,5,7 are administered in person. Interviews 2,4,6 are administered by telephone.
1981	*Measuring Crime* is released, inaugurating BJS bulletin series. The publication compares NCS and UCR methodologies and measures.
	CSRC conducts first test of new screening strategies to elicit reports of victimizations in Peoria reverse record check study. First application of Computer Assisted Telephone interviewing (CATI) methods to NCS.
1982-83	Longitudinal Task Force, created by CSRC, studies feasibility of adopting longitudinal design for NCS.

Year	Design Change
1983	BJS created Implementation Task Force to evaluate proposed changes emerging from CSRC work and to advise on strategies for adopting revisions in operation NCS environment. Proposed changes are divided into two groups, depending on their expected likelihood for affecting crime rates. Near-term changes (judged non-rate-affecting) were implemented simultaneously in 1986. Long-term changes (rate-affecting) were later implemented together.
1984	Phase in of revised Primary Sampling Units (PSU) design begins. PSU sample designs are updated by Census to reflect results of the 1980 Census. Beginning in 1984 both 1970 and 1980 Census sample designs are used in drawing the sample of housing units.
	The overall number of PSUs is reduced from 220 Non-self Representing (NSR) to 153 NSRs. This change results in a 20% sample reduction in the largest of the 156 self-representing (SR) PSUs. The 1980 design consists of 84 SR and 153 NSR PSUs. This constitutes a 15% decline in sample size and was implemented to provide funds for redesign testing and phase-in at the Bureau of the Census.
1985	Census Bureau opens provisional CATI interviewing facility in Hagerstown, MD. NCS is the first federally-sponsored survey program to evaluate use of CATI for data collection and to utilize this facility.
	CSRC conducts split-ballot test, comparing revised screener and current NCS vehicle, using national RDD sample. Revised screener produced a net increase of 28% more victimization reports.
	Non-rate affecting changes are introduced to a partial sample.
1986	Redesigned sample based on 1980 Decennial Census is introduced. Incorporates stratifiers based on UCR jurisdiction-level data. Public use tape record Ids are scrambled to preserve confidentiality.
	BJS finalized long-term, rate-affecting revisions to NCS and communicates these decisions to Census Bureau.
	12 and 13 year olds are now interviewed directly.

Year	Design Change
1986	Proportion of NCS phone interviews is increased from 50% to 75%. Interviews 1 and 5 are still conducted in person.
	Near-term changes are implemented.
1987	Census Bureau begins phase-in of CATI for cases drawn from actual NCS sample at Hagerstown (400 cases). Pretest of long-term NCS revisions is conducted in Washington, D.C.
	A total sample of 49,000 housing units is selected. Approximately 3,400 of these households are interviewed using Computer Assisted Telephone Interviewing (CATI). These estimates are excluded from reports until the effect of CATI on estimates is examined. Weights are applied to control for these omitted cases.
	Non-rate affecting changes are introduced to full sample.
1988	A total sample of 50,000 housing units is selected. Of this sample approximately 5%, or 2,500, households are interviewed using CATI. Previous examination of CATI estimates shows that there is no significant difference between these estimates and telephone interviewing. Data using the CATI estimates is included in the 1988 victimization estimates.
	75% of interviews are done by telephone.
1989	Census Bureau begins phase-in of long-term changes. Random 5% of NCS sample receives long-term questionnaire.
	A total sample of 62,700 housing units is selected for inclusion in the survey. Of these households 58,800 are designated as the "near term sample" and are administered the original questionnaire. The near term sample is comprised of 97,000 persons in 48,400 occupied households. CATI was used for interviewing of 5% of the near term sample.
	A sub-sample of 3,800 households is selected to receive a revised questionnaire. The revised form sample is comprised of 6,000 persons in 3,100 households. The revised instrument is designed to broaden the scope of incidents covered and includes the offense of vandalism.

Year	Design Change
1990	A total sample of 62,600 housing is units is selected. Of these households 56,800 are administered the original questionnaire. The near term sample is comprised of approximately 95,000 persons in 47,000 occupied households.
	A sub-sample of 5,700 households is selected to receive the revised questionnaire. Approximately 9,000 persons in 4,700 occupied households are interviewed. This data is excluded from the victimization estimates for the year, and weights are applied to control for these omitted cases.
	CATI is used for 10% of the near term sample.
1991	Rape and sexual assault screener items are revised in long-term questionnaire. CATI first used with long-term questionnaire on these cases.
	Survey name changed to National Crime Victimization Survey (NCVS). Subsequent discussion results in name National Crime Survey being used for data collected prior to long-term changes, National Crime Victimization Survey afterwards.
	A total sample of 50,500 housing units is selected. Approximately 50,500 households are administered the NCS survey as the near term sample. The sample consists of 83,500 persons in 41,700 occupied households. Ten percent of the near term sample is interviewed using CATI.
	A sub-sample of 10,500 households is selected to receive the revised questionnaire with a total of 21,000 persons being interviewed. This data is excluded from the victimization estimates for the year, and weights are applied to control for these omitted cases.
	CATI is used for 10%, or approximately 4,170 households, of the near term sample telephone interviews.
	75% of interviews are now done by telephone.

Year	Design Change
1992	A total sample of 60,500 households is selected. A sub-sample of 28,700 households is selected to receive the revised questionnaire with 23,900 persons being surveyed. This data is excluded from the victimization estimates for the year, and weights are applied to control for these omitted cases.
	The remaining near term sample of 31,800 households and 26,200 individuals are administered the original survey.
	CATI is used for 10%, or approximately 2,620 households, of the near term sample telephone interviews.
1993	A split sample is used between 1992-1993. The 50-50 split occurred over an eighteen-month period and was designed to allow for comparative analyses between the old and new questionnaire.
	From January – June approximately 28,700 households are designated to be in the half-sample test of the redesigned survey.
	Beginning in July of 1993 the entire sample of 58,710 households are administered the redesigned survey.
	CATI is used for 30%, or approximately 14,481 households, of the telephone interviews.
	Sample PSUs now fall into three distinct categories of CATI usage. Maximum CATI refers to PSUs in which all segments are eligible for CATI. Half-CATI and No-CATI comprise the remaining two groups.
1994	The full sample is administered the redesigned survey.
	Approximately 14,280 households are surveyed using CATI procedures.
	First data utilizing new, long-term procedures received for producing annual change estimates.
1995	Sampled households are drawn from both the 1980 and 1990 Census based PSUs. The 1990 design consists of 92 SR and 153 NSR PSUs.
	14,250 households are surveyed using CATI procedures.

Year	Design Change
1996	The Bureau of Justice Statistics begins using collection year data for the estimation of victimization rates in the yearly Bulletin. This allows for more timely release of estimates for the previous year. Data year data are still in use for the Tomes and Statistical Abstract Tables.
2002	New OMB designations for race are mandated by Congress. Under the new reporting respondents to all government surveys may identify as multi-racial. These new racial categories will create a break in the NCVS series since the new reporting system means that racial categories for pre-2003 and post 2003 will not be comparable

Source: Bureau of Justice Statistics, 1993, Criminal Victimization in the United States, Appendix 5,

APPENDIX 3

Bivariate correlation matrix for dependent variables and police organization variables

	(1)	(2)	(3)	(4)	(5)	(6)	(7)	(8)
(1) Year								
(2) Rape	.868**							
(3) Robbery	.759**	.431*						
(4) Aggravated assault	.942**	.775**	.769**					
(5) UCR coverage	-.668**	-.710**	-.357	-.578**				
(6) NIBRS	-.805**	.783**	.457*	.858**	-.592**			
(7) Arrest ratio	-.944**	-.866**	-.669**	-.895**	.713**	-.807**		
(8) % 911	.975**	.920**	.659**	.910**	-.736**	.840**	-.937**	
(9) % civilian	.941**	.721**	.836**	.861**	-.527	.606**	-.834**	.864**
(10) LEMAS in field	.939**	.828**	-.768**	.589	-.674*	.842**	-.909**	.981**
(11) LEMAS record keeping	.797**	.865**	-.789**	.388	-.744**	.647*	-.813**	.887**
(12) LEMAS crim. investig.	.798**	.883**	-.818**	.348	-.719*	.639*	-.771**	.908**
(13) LEMAS arrest	.966**	.843**	-.815**	.604*	-.680*	.880*	-.910**	.999**
(14) LEMAS warrants	.970**	.852**	-.828**	.621*	-.715*	.888**	-.938**	.992**
(15) LEMAS personal	.997**	.891**	-.914**	.618	-.777**	.977**	-.925**	.976**

	(9)	(10)	(11)	(12)	(13)	(14)	(15)
(1) Year							
(2) Rape							
(3) Robbery							
(4) Aggravated assault							
(5) UCR coverage							
(6) NIBRS							
(7) Arrest ratio							
(8) % 911							
(9) % civilian							
(10) LEMAS in field	.158						
(11) LEMAS record keeping	.000	.936**					
(12) LEMAS crim. investig.	.007	.942**	.982**				
(13) LEMAS arrest	.275	.986**	.900**	.921**			
(14) LEMAS warrants	.306	.979**	.913**	.914***	.992**		
(15) LEMAS personal	.388	.922**	.878**	.884**	.969**	.982**	

APPENDIX 4

Bivariate correlation matrix for dependent variables and social attitude variables used in the first stage of the analysis

	(1)	(2)	(3)	(4)	(5)	(6)	(7)	(8)
(1) Year								
(2) Rape	.868**							
(3) Robbery	.759**	.431*						
(4) Agg. assault	.942**	.775**	.769**					
(5) Police ethics	.778**	.653**	.555**	.791**				
(6) Conf. in police	.613**	.528*	.088	.613**	.718**			
(7) Not okay to strike	.826**	.720**	.620**	.819**	.688**	.631**		
(8) Courts harsh enough	.545**	.554**	.221	.632**	.811**	.825**	.675**	
(9) Beyond cohab.	.977**	.756**	.811**	.920**	.718**	-.128	-.764**	-.461*
(10) Warrantless arrest	.985**	.776**	.820**	.947**	.678**	-.165	-.778**	-.463*
(11) No contact PO	.965**	.751**	.787**	.910**	.714**	-.006	-.764**	-.463*
(12) Custody relief	.904**	.630**	.804**	.854**	.749**	-.072	-.704**	-.387
(13) Misd. po viol.	.994**	.836**	.749**	.926**	.618**	-.079	-.793**	-.538**
(14) Civil/ criminal	.816**	.529*	.754**	.765**	.751**	.112	-.623**	-.297
(15) Felony po viol.	.791**	.933**	.306	.702**	.444*	.190	-.588**	-.498*
(16) Mand. arrest	.970**	.888**	.672**	.924**	.515*	-.066	-.782**	-.577**
(17) Firearm confis.	.799**	.925**	.324	.729**	.353	.190	-.647**	-.603**

	(9)	(10)	(11)	(12)	(13)	(14)	(15)	(16)
(1) Year								
(2) Rape								
(3) Robbery								
(4) Agg. assault								
(5) Police ethics								
(6) Conf. in police								
(7) Not okay to strike								
(8) Courts harsh enough								
(9) Beyond cohab.								
(10) Warrantless arrest	.989**							
(11) No contact PO	.988**	.980**						
(12) Custody relief	.964**	.946**	.981**					
(13) Misd. po viol.	.974**	.982**	.966**	.907**				
(14) Civil/ criminal	.900**	.872**	.935***	.980***	.819**			
(15) Felony po viol.	.679**	.708***	.705***	.584***	.780**	.510*		
(16) Mand. arrest	.903**	.931**	.882**	.785***	.964***	.665**	.835**	
(17) Firearm confis.	.668**	.699**	.669**	.526*	.792**	.410	.949**	.888**

APPENDIX 5

Bivariate correlation matrix for dependent variables and NCVS design-related variables used in the first stage of the analysis

	(1)	(2)	(3)	(4)	(5)	(6)	(7)	(8)	(9)	(10)	(11)
(1) Year											
(2) Rape	.868**										
(3) Robbery	.759**	.431*									
(4) Aggravated assault	.942**	.775**	.769**								
(5) Change in proxy interviews	.859**	.721**	.754**	.800**							
(6) PSU reduction	.835**	.638**	.781**	.743**	.870**						
(7) Redesign	.794**	.902**	.328	.768**	.572**	.498**					
(8) Person response rate	-.935**	-.931**	-.541**	-.908**	-.735**	-.693**	-.924**				
(9) Percent CATI	.886**	.936**	.496**	.823**	.732**	.637**	.903**	-.937**			
(10) Percent telephone	.890**	.695**	.808**	.797**	.898**	.881**	.529**	-.720**	.675**		
(11) Household response rate	-.715**	-.808**	-.267	-.759**	-.469**	-.417*	-.877*	.872**	-.793**	-.414*	

APPENDIX 6

Results of factor analyses for variables used in the first stage of the analysis

FACTOR NAME

UCR Technology

Component	Mean	Std. Dev.	Description	Factor Loading	Factor Score
UCR coverage	88.94	3.99	population covered by UCR	.965	.932
Percent civilian	20.39	2.48	civilian employees in police depts.	.965	.932

Pearson's Correlation Matrix

	(1)	(2)
(1) UCR coverage	1.000	
(5) % civilian	.864**	

Cronbach's Alpha Coefficient of Reliability = .93

Appendix 6, continued

FACTOR NAME

Police Organization LEMAS (computer usage variables)

Component	Mean	Std. Dev.	Description
In field	49.25	9.34	in field calls for service
Records	59.45	10.08	function record keeping
Investigation	43.30	7.62	function criminal investigation
Arrest	58.26	11.02	function arrest management
Warrants	38.30	4.69	function warrants management
Personal	58.67	12.09	percent using personal computers

Pearson Correlation Matrix

	(1)	(2)	(3)	(4)	(5)	(6) Factor Loading	Factor Score
(1)In field	1.000					.995	.172
(2)Records	.936**	1.000				.976	.168
(3)Investigation	.942**	.982**	1.000			.980	.169
(4)Arrest	.986**	.900**	.921**	1.000		.995	.172
(5)Warrants	.979**	.913**	.914**	.992**	1.000	.993	.171
(6)Personal	.923**	.878**	.884**	.969**	.982**	1.000 .956	.165

Cronbach's Alpha Coefficient of Reliability = .98

FACTOR NAME

Social Attitudes GSS (feelings toward the criminal justice system and officials)

Component	Mean	Std. Dev.	Description
Ethics	48.23	6.28	% respondent feeling ethics of police are very high/high
Conf. protect	52.63	6.19	% respondents with confidence in ability of police to protect
Not okay to hit	30.23	3.83	% imagine a situation where it's okay for police to strike citizen
Courts	21.02	5.83	% stating courts are too harsh on criminals

	Factor Loading	Factor Score
	.877	.278
	.898	.285
	.824	.261
	.947	.301

Pearson Correlation Matrix

	(1)	(2)	(3)	(4)
(1) Ethics	1.00			
(2) Conf. protect	.718**	1.000		
(3) Not okay to hit	.688**	.631**	1.000	
(4) Courts okay	.811**	.825**	.675**	.000

Cronbach's Alpha Coefficient of Reliability = .90

199

Appendix 6, continued

FACTOR NAME

Social Attitudes Domestic Violence Legislation

Component	Mean	Std. Dev.	Description
Bey. Cohab.	56.95	32.13	eligibility for protection beyond cohabitating couples
Warrantless	60.96	32.82	police may arrest without a warrant
No contact	60.87	28.17	no contact protection orders available
Custody	63.37	29.01	victim custody relief
Mid. PO	41.27	27.33	misdemeanor for parole violation
Contempt	53.30	20.55	civil or criminal contempt for protection order violation
Felony PO	2.76	2.15	felony charge for protection order violation
Mandatory	26.38	21.87	mandatory arrest for domestic violence
Firearm	9.63	15.94	confiscation of firearm for protection order violation

Pearson Correlation Matrix

	(1)	(2)	(3)	(4)	(5)	(6)	(7)	(8)	(9)
(1) Bey. Cohab.	1.000								
(2) Warrantless	.989**	1.000							
(3) No contact	.988	.980**	1.000						
(4) Custody	.964**	.946**	.981**	1.000					
(5) Mid. PO	.974**	.982**	.966**	.907	1.000				
(6) Contempt	.900**	.872**	.935**	.980**	.819**	1.000			
(7) Felony PO	.679**	.708**	.705**	.584**	.780**	.510*	1.000		
(8) Mandatory	.903**	.931**	.882*	.785**	.964**	.665**	.835**	1.000	
(9) Firearm	.668**	.699**	.669**	.526*	.792**	.410	.949**	.888**	1.000

Social Attitudes Domestic Violence Legislation, cont.

	Factor 1		Factor 2	
	Rotated Factor Loading	Factor Score	Rotated Factor Loading	Factor Score
Eligibility beyond cohabitation		.872	-.164	.472
Warrantless arrest okay	.983	.842	-.108	.519
No contact PO	.983	.883	-.175	.466
Victim custody relief	.933	.951	-.349	.297
Misdemeanor for PO violation	.990	.766	-.003	.628
Civil or criminal contempt	.864	.961	-.454	.172
Felony for PO violation	.804	.313	.525	.908
Mandatory arrest for PO violation	.947	.598	.244	.774
Firearm confiscation	.787	.247	.609	.963

Cronbach's Alpha Coefficient of Reliability = Factor 1: .98   Factor 2: .97

Appendix 6, continued

FACTOR NAME

Social Attitudes Domestic Violence Legislation, cont.

	Factor 1		Factor 2	
	Rotated Factor Loading	Factor Score	Rotated Factor Loading	Factor Score
Eligibility beyond cohabitation	.	.872	-.164	.472
Warrantless arrest okay	.983	.842	-.108	.519
No contact PO	.983	.883	-.175	.466
Victim custody relief	.933	.951	-.349	.297
Misdemeanor for PO violation	.990	.766	-.003	.628
Civil or criminal contempt	.864	.961	-.454	.172
Felony for PO violation	.804	.313	.525	.908
Mandatory arrest for PO violation	.947	.598	.244	.774
Firearm confiscation	.787	.247	.609	.963

Cronbach's Alpha Coefficient of Reliability = Factor 1: .98   Factor 2: .97

FACTOR NAME

NCVS Response

Component	Mean	Std. Dev.	Description	Factor Loading	Factor Score
Person	94.69	3.52	percentage of sampled persons responding to the survey	.968	.936
Household	95.42	1.25	percentage of sampled households responding to the survey	.968	.936

Pearson's Correlation Matrix

	(1)	(2)
(1) Person	1.000	
(4) Household	.872**	

Cronbach's Alpha Coefficient of Reliability = .93

NCVS Technology

Component	Mean	Std. Dev.	Description	Factor Loading	Factor Score
% CATI	11.33	13.77	percentage of interviews conducted with CATI	.915	.837
% telephone	56.87	22.8	percentage of interviews conducted by telephone	.915	.837

Pearson's Correlation Matrix

	(1)	(2)
(1)% CATI	1.000	
(4)% telephone	.675	

Cronbach's Alpha Coefficient of Reliability = .81

APPENDIX 7

Bivariate correlation matrix for dependent variables and factor scores used in the first stage of the analysis

	(1)	(2)	(3)	(4)	(5)	(6)	(7)	(8)	(9)	(10)	(11)
(1) UCR technology											
(2) Arrest ratio	-.918*										
(3) UCR population covered	-.655**	.713**									
(4) Feelings toward CJ	.768**	-.811**	-.614**								
(5) Victim oriented legislation	.655**	-.504*	-.424*	-.088							
(6) Offender oriented legislation	.713**	-.723**	-.698**	.633**	.000						
(7) NCVS response	-.808**	.863**	.664**	.664**	-.834**	-.189					
(8) NCVS technology	.970**	-.918**	-.710**	.641**	.615**	.734**	-.891**				
(9) NCVS change in proxy interview	.861**	-.867**	-.619*	.429*	.574**	.547**	-.622**	.891**			
(10) NCVS PSU reduction	.840**	-.819**	-.666**	.422	.710**	.409	-.574**	.829**	.870**		
(11) NCVS redesign		.755**	-.800**	-.660**	.711**	.078	.915**	-.931**	.783**	.572**	.498**

References

Aderholt, Robert B. *Congressional House of Representatives,* Thursday May 27, 1999.

Akiyama, Yoshio and Harvey Rosenthal. 1990. "The future of the uniform crime reporting program: Its scope and promise." In Doris Mackenzie, Phyllis Baunach, and Roy Roberg (eds). *Measuring Crime: Large-Scale, Long-Range Efforts* (pp. 4-74). Albany, NY: State University of New York Press.

Akiyama, Yoshio and James Nolan. 1999. "Methods for understanding and analyzing NIBRS data." *Journal of Quantitative Criminology,* 15:225-238.

Atrostic, B. K., Nancy Bates, Geraldine Burt, and Adriana Silberstein. 2001. "Nonresponse in U.S. government household surveys: consistent measures, recent trends, and new insights." *Journal of Official Statistics,* 17:209-226.

Baker, Mary, Barbara Nienstedt, Ronald Everett, and Richard McCleary. 1983. "The impact of a crime wave: perceptions, fear and confidence in the police." *Law and Society Review,* 17:319-335.

Baumer, Eric, Richard Felson, and Steven Messner. 2003. "Changes in police notification for rape, 1973-2000." *Criminology,* 23:841-872.

Biderman, Albert and James Lynch. 1991. *Understanding crime incidence statistics: Why the UCR diverges from the NCS.* New York: Springer-Verlag.

Biderman, Albert and David Cantor. 1984. "A longitudinal analysis of bounding, respondent conditioning and mobility as sources of panel bias in the National Crime Survey." Proceedings of the Section for Survey Research Methods, American Statistical Association.

Berger, Ronald, Lawrence Neuman, and Patricia Searles. 1994. "The impact of rape law reform: An aggregate analysis of police reports and arrests." *Criminal Justice Review,* 19:1-23.

Black, Donald. 1970. "Production of crime rates." *American Sociological Review,* 35:733-758.

Blumstein, Albert. 2000a.The recent rise and fall of American violence. In Albert Blumstein and Joel Wallman (eds). *The Crime Drop in America* (pp. 1-12). Cambridge: Cambridge University Press.

_____. 2000b. Disaggregating the violence trends. In Alfred Blumstein and Joel Wallman (eds.) *The Crime Drop in America* (pp. 13-44). Cambridge: Cambridge University Press.

_____. 1998. Violence certainly is the problem- and especially with handguns. *University of Colorado Law Review,* 69:945-967.

_____. 1995. "Violence by young people: Why the deadly nexus?" *National Institute of Justice Journal* (pp. 2-9). August.

Blumstein, Alfred, Jacqueline Cohen and Richard Rosenfeld. 1991. "Trend and deviation in crime rates: A comparison of UCR and NCS data for burglary and robbery." *Criminology,* 29:237-263.

Blumstein, Albert and Richard Rosenfeld. 1998. "Exploring recent trends in U.S. homicide rates." *Journal of Criminal Law and Criminology,* 88:1175-1216.

Browne, Angela. 1987. *When Battered Women Kill.* New York: Free Press.

Brownmiller, Susan. 1975. *Against Our Will: Men, Women, and Rape.* New York: Simon and Schuster.

Cahalan, Margaret. 1986. *Historical Corrections Statistics in the United States, 1850-1984.* U.S. Department of Justice, Bureau of Justice Statistics. Washington, DC: U.S. Government Printing Office.

Chilton, Roland. 1986. "Age, sex, race, and arrest trends for 12 of the nation's largest central cities." In J.M. Byrne and R.J. Sampson (eds). *The Social Ecology of Crime* (pp. 102-115). New York: Springer-Verlag.

Chilton, Roland and John Jarvis. 1999. "Using the National Incident-Based Reporting System (NIBRS) to test estimates of arrestee and offender characteristics." *Journal of Quantitative Criminology* 15:207-224.

Chilton, Roland and John Jarvis. 1999. "Victims and offenders in two crime statistics programs: A comparison of the National Incident-

Based Reporting System (NIBRS) and the National Crime Victimization Survey (NCVS)." *Journal of Quantitative Criminology,* 15:193-206.

Cohen, Lawrence E., David Cantor and James R. Kluegel. 1981. "Robbery victimization in the U.S.: An analysis of a nonrandom event." *Social Sciences Quarterly,* 4:645-657.

Cohen, Lawrence and Kenneth Land. 1987. "Age structure and crime: Symmetry versus asymmetry and the projection of crime rates through the 1990's." *American Sociological Review,* 52:170-183.

_____. 1984. "Discrepancies between crime reports and crime surveys: Urban and structural determinants." *Criminology,* 22:499-530.

Cohen, Larry J. and Mark I. Lichbach. 1982. "Alternative measures of crime: A statistical evaluation." *Sociological Quarterly,* 23:253-266.

Cohen, Lawrence E and Marcus Felson. 1979. "Social change and crime rate trends: A routine activity approach." *American Sociological Review,* 44:588-608.

Cohen, Lawrence E., Marcus Felson, Kenneth C. Land. 1980. "Property crime rates in the United States: A macrodynamic analysis, 1947-1977; with Ex Ante forecasts for the mid-1980s." *American Journal of Sociology,* 86:90-118.

Conaway, Mark and Sharon Lohr. 1994. "A longitudinal analysis of factors associated with reporting violent crimes to the police." *Journal of Quantitative Criminology,* 3:23-39.

Crowell, Nancy and Ann W. Burgess. 1996. *Understanding Violence Against Women.* Washington: National Academy Press.

Dodge, Richard. 1987. *Series Crimes: Report of a Field Test Technical Report.* Washington DC: Bureau of Justice Statistics. NCJ 104615.

Dugan, Laura. 2003. "Domestic violence legislation: Exploring its impact on the likelihood of domestic violence, police involvement, and arrest." *Criminology and Public Policy,* 2:283-309.

Dugan, Laura. 1999. "The effect of criminal victimization on a household's moving decision." *Criminology,* 37:903-930.

Dugan, Laura, Daniel Nagin, and Richard Rosenfeld. 2003. "Exposure reduction or retaliation? The effects of domestic violence resources on intimate-partner homicide." *Law and Society Review,* 37:169-198.

Dunn, Christopher and Thomas Zelenock. 1999. "NIBRS data available for secondary analysis." *Journal of Quantitative Criminology,* 15:239-248.

Ericson, Richard and Kevin Haggerty. 1997. *Policing the Risk Society.* Toronto: University of Toronto Press.

Federal Bureau of Investigation. *Crime in the United States, 1973-2002.* Washington, DC Government Printing Office.

Federal Bureau of Investigation. 1984. *Uniform Crime Reporting Handbook.* Washington, DC Government Printing Office.

Fox, James. 2000. Demographics and U.S. homicide. In Alfred Blumstein and Joel Wallman (eds). *The Crime Drop in America* (pp. 288-317). Cambridge: Cambridge University Press.

_____. 1996. *Trends in Juvenile Violence.* Washington DC: U.S. Department of Justice. BJS Report NCJ 170379 and 170377.

Groves, Robert and Mick Couper. 1998. *Nonresponse in Household Interview Surveys.* New York: John Wiley and Sons, Inc.

Gottfredson, Michael and Don Gottfredson. 1980. *Decisionmaking in Criminal Justice.* Cambridge: Ballinger.

Gottfredson, Michael and Michael Hindelang. 1979. "A study of the behavior of law." *American Sociological Review,* 44:3-17.

Gove, Walter, Michael Hughes, and Michael Geerken. 1985. "Are uniform crime reports a valid indicator of index crimes: An affirmative answer with minor qualifications." *Criminology,* 23:451-501.

Gugarati, Damodar. 1995. *Basic Econometrics.* New York: McGraw Hill.

Hamilton, James D. 1994. *Time Series Analysis.* New Jersey: Princeton University Press.

Hart, Timothy and Callie Rennison. 2003. *Reporting Crime to the Police.* Bureau of Justice Statistics. Washington, DC: U.S. Government Printing Office. NCJ 195710.

Harris, Anthony, Stephen Thomas, Gene Fisher, and David Hirsch. 2002. "Murder and medicine: The lethality of criminal assault 1960-1999." *Homicide Studies,* 6:128-166.

Hindelang, Michael and Michael Gottfredson. 1976. "The criminal justice system: Public attitudes and involvement." In W. McDonald (ed). *Criminal Justice and the Victim.* Beverly Hills: Sage.

Hindelang, Michael, Michael Gottfredson and James Garofalo. 1978. *Victims of Personal Crime: An Empirical Foundation for a Theory of Personal Victimization.* Cambridge: Ballinger Publishing Company.

Hindelang, Michael, Travis Hirschi, and Joseph Weis. 1979. "Correlates of delinquency: The illusion of discrepancy between self-report and official measures." *American Sociological Review,* 44:995-1014.

Jensen, Gary and Mary Altani Karpos. 1993. "Managing rape: exploratory research on the behavior of rape statistics." *Criminology,* 31:363-385.

Johnston, Jack and John DiNardo. 1997. *Econometric Methods.* New York: McGraw-Hill.

Kincaid, Stephen. 1984. Oregon UCR Crime Statistics, July 1984. *Blueprint for the Future of the Uniform Crime Reporting Program.* pg. 86. cited in Akiyama and Rosenthal.

Kinderman, Charles, James Lynch, and David Cantor. 1997. *Effects of the Redesign on Victimization Estimates.* Washington DC: U.S. Department of Justice. BJS Fact Sheet NCJ 164381.

Kitsuse, John and Aaron Cicourel. 1963. "A note on the use of official statistics." *Social Problems,* 11:131-38.

LaFree, Gary and Kriss Drass. 2002. "Counting crime booms among nations: Evidence for homicide victimization rates, 1959-1998." *Criminology,* 40:769-799.

Langan, Patrick A. and David Farrington. 1998. *Crime and Justice in the United States and in England and Wales, 1981-1996.* Washington DC: U.S. Department of Justice. BJS Report NCJ 169284.

Langworthy, Robert. 2002. "LEMAS: A comparative organizational research platform." *Justice and Research Policy,* 4:21-38.

Langworthy, Robert. 1999. *Measuring what matters: Proceedings from the policing research institute meetings.* Washington, DC: National Institute of Justice.

Levitt, Steven. 1998. "The relationship between crime reporting and police: Implications for the use of uniform crime reports." *Journal of Quantitative Criminology* 14:61-81.

Lott, John. 1998. *More Guns, Less Crime.* Chicago: University of Chicago Press.

Lott, John and D. Mustard. 1997. "Crime, deterrence, and right-to-carry concealed handguns." *Journal of Legal Studies,* 26:1-68.

Maguire, Edward. 2002. "Multiwave establishment surveys of police organizations." *Justice Research Policy,* 4:39-59.

Maguire, Edward, J. Snipes, M. Townsend, and C. Uchida. 1998. "Counting cops: Estimating the number of police departments and police officers in the United States." *Policing: An International Journal of Police Strategies and Management,* 21:97-120.

Maltz, Michael. 1999. *Bridging Gaps in Police Crime Data.* Washington DC: U.S. Department of Justice. BJS Report NCJ 176365.

Maltz, Michael and Joseph Targonski. 2002. "A note on the use of county level UCR data." *Journal of Quantitative Criminology,* 18:297-318.

Martin, E. 1981. "A twist on the Heisenberg Principal: Or, how crime affects it's measurement." *Social Indicators Research,* 9:197-223.

Martin, S. 1995. "A cross-burning is not just an arson: Police social construction of hate crimes in Baltimore County." *Criminology,* 33:303-326.

Maxfield, Michael. 1999. "The National Incident-Based Reporting System: Research and policy applications." *Journal of Quantitative Criminology,* 15:119-150.

McCleary, Richard, Barbara Bienstadt, and James Erven. 1982. "Uniform Crime Reports as organization outcomes: Three time series experiments." *Social Problems,* 29:361-367.

McDowall, David and Colin Loftin. 1992. "Comparing the UCR and NCS over time." *Criminology,* 30:125-132.

Menard, Scott. 1992. "Residual gains, reliability, and the UCR-NCS relationship: A comment on Blumstein, Cohen, and Rosenfeld (1991)." *Criminology,* 30:105-113.

_____. 1991. "Encouraging news for criminologists (in the year 2050)? A comment on O'Brien (1990)." *Journal of Criminal Justice,* 19:563-567.

Menard, Scott and Herbert Covey. 1988. "UCR and NCS: Comparisons over space and time." *Journal of Criminal Justice,* 16:371-384.

O'Brien, Robert. 1999a. "The enduring effects of cohort characteristics on age-specific homicide rates, 1960-1995." *American Journal of Sociology,* 4:1061-1095.

_____, 1999b. "Measuring the convergence/divergence of "serious crime" arrest rates for males and females: 1960-1995." *Journal of Quantitative Criminology,* 15:97-114.

_____. 1996. "Police productivity and crime rates: 1973-1992." *Criminology,* 34:183-207.

_____. 1991. "Detrended UCR and NCS crime rates: Their utility and meaning." *Journal of Criminal Justice,* 19:569-574.

_____. 1990. "Comparing detrended UCR and NCS crime rates over time: 1973-1986." *Journal of Criminal Justice,* 18:229-238.

O'Brien, Robert, David Shichor and David L. Decker. 1980. "An empirical comparison of the validity of UCR and NCS crime rates." *Sociological Quarterly,* 21:391-401.

Ostrom, Charles. 1978. *Time Series Analysis: Regression Techniques.* Beverly Hills: Sage Publications.

Parks, Roger. 1976. "Police response to victimization: Effects on citizen attitudes and perceptions." In Wesley Skogan (ed). *Sample Surveys of the Victims of Crime* (pp. 89-104). Cambridge, MA: Ballinger Publishing Company.

Penick, Bettye and Maurice Owens (eds). 1976. *Surveying Crime. A Report of the Panel for the Evaluation of Crime Surveys.* Washington, D.C.: Washington National Academy of Science.

Pindyck, Robert S. and Daniel L. Rubinfeld. 1998. *Econometric Models and Economic Forecasts.* Boston: Irwin/McGraw Hill.

President's Commission. 1967. *Task Force Report: Crime and Its Impact: An Assessment. President's Commission on Law Enforcement and the Administration of Justice.* Washington DC: U.S. Government Printing Office.

Rand, Michael, James Lynch, and David Cantor. 1997. *Criminal Victimization, 1973-1995.* Washington D.C. U.S. Government Printing Office. NCJ 163069.

Rand, Michael and Callie Rennison. 2002. *True Crime Stories? Accounting for Differences in Our National Crime Indicators.* Window on Washington. Washington DC: U.S. Government Printing Office.

Rantala, Ramona. 2000. *The Effects of NIBRS on Crime Statistics.* Bureau of Justice Statistics. Washington, DC: U.S. Government Printing Office. NCJ 178890.

Reiss, Albert and Jeffrey Roth (eds). 1993. *Understanding and Preventing Violence.* Washington, DC: National Academy Press.

Reiss, A. 1967. *Measurement of the nature and amount of crime: Studies in crime and law enforcement in major metropolitan areas.* (vol. 1: Field Surveys III). Washington, DC: Government Printing Office.

Rosenfeld, Richard. 2004. *The UCR-NCVS Convergence and Changes in Police Recording of Assaults.* Paper presented at the spring NCOVR workshop, Washington, DC. March, 2004.

Rosenfeld, Richard. 2000. "Patterns in adult homicide: 1980-1995." In Alfred Blumstein and Joel Wallman (eds). *The Crime Drop in America* (pp. 130-163). Cambridge: Cambridge University Press.

Schneider, Victoria and Brian Wiersema. 1990. "Limits and use of the Uniform Crime Reports." In Doris Mackenzie, Phyllis Baunach, and Roy Roberg (eds). *Measuring Crime: Large-Scale, Long-Range Efforts* (pp. 21-48). Albany: State University of New York Press.

Sherman, Lawrence. 1992. *Policing Domestic Violence Experiments and Dilemmas.* New York: The Free Press.

Sherman, Lawrence and Richard Berk. 1984. The specific deterrent effects of arrest for domestic assault. *American Sociological Review,* 49:261-272.

Skogan, Wesley. 1984. "Reporting crimes to the police: The status of world research." *Journal of Research in Crime and Delinquency,* 21:113-137.

_____. 1975. "Measurement problems in official and survey crime rates." *Journal of Criminal Justice,* 3:17-32.

SPSS 12.0. 2003. SPSS Inc.

Sourcebook of Criminal Justice Statistics, 1975-2002.

Sparks, Richard F. 1981. "Surveys of victimization: An optimistic assessment." In Michael Tonry and Norval Morris (eds). *Crime and Justice An Annual Review of Research,* vol. 3 (pp. 1-60). Chicago: University of Chicago Press.

Sparks, Richard. 1976. "Crimes and Victims in London." In Wesley Skogan (ed). *Sample Surveys of the Victims of Crime* (pp. 43-71). Cambridge, MA: Ballinger Publishing Company.

Stamp, Sir Josiah. 1929. *Some Economic Factors in Modern Life.* London: P.S. King and Son, Ltd.

Swanson, Greg. 2002. *NIBRS Status Report 2002.* NIBRS Implementation Coordinator. Federal Bureau of Investigation.

Thompson, Martie, Linda Saltzman and Daniel Bibel. 1999. "Applying NIBRS data to the study of intimate partner violence: Massachusetts as a case study." *Journal of Quantitative Criminology,* 15:163-180.

United States Department of Justice. 2002. *Four Measures of Serious Violent Crime.* Washington DC: U.S. Department of Justice. BJS Fact Sheet. http://www.ojp.usdoj.gov/bjs/glance/cv2.htm. December 31, 2002.

United States Department of Justice. 2002a. *National Incident Based Reporting System (NIBRS) Implementation Program.* Washington DC: U.S. Department of Justice. http://www.ojp.usdoj.gov/bjs/nibrs.htm.

United States Department of Justice, Bureau of Justice Statistics. *Prisoners in 2000.* Washington, DC: U.S. Government Printing Office.

United States Department of Justice, Bureau of Justice Statistics. *Law Enforcement Management and Administrative Statistics (LEMAS): 1987-2000.* Washington DC: U.S. Government Printing Office.

United States Department of Justice, Federal Bureau of Investigation. *National Incident-Based Reporting System, 1991-2000.* Compiled by the U.S. Dept. of Justice, Federal Bureau of Investigation. ICPSR ed. Ann Arbor, MI: Inter-university Consortium for Political and Social Research [producer and distributor], 2002.

United States Department of Justice. Bureau of Justice Statistics. *Criminal Victimization in the United States, 1973-1994.* Washington, DC: U.S. Government Printing Office.

United States Department of Justice. Bureau of Justice Statistics. *Criminal Victimization in the United States, Statistical Tables, 1996-2002.* http://www.ojp.usdoj.gov/bjs/abstract/cvusst.htm

United States Department of Justice. Federal Bureau of Investigation. *Crime in the United States, 1973-2002.* Washington, DC: U.S. Government Printing Office.

United States Department of Justice. 2000. *The Nation's Two Crime Measures.* Washington DC: U.S. Department of Justice. BJS Fact Sheet NCJ 122795.

United States Department of Justice. 1998. *Building Knowledge About Crime and Justice, Research Prospectus.* Washington DC: National Institute of Justice. NCJ 167570.

Index